MICHAEL WEBER

CONFESSIONS
OF AN INTERNET AUCTION JUNKIE

HOW TO SELL VIRTUALLY ANYTHING ON THE INTERNET

PRIMA
TECH

Send Us Your Comments:

To comment on this book or any other PRIMA TECH title, visit our reader response page on the Web at www.prima-tech.com/comments.

How to Order:

For information on quantity discounts, contact the publisher: Prima Publishing, P.O. Box 1260BK, Rocklin, CA 95677-1260; (916) 787-7000. On your letterhead, include information concerning the intended use of the books and the number of books you want to purchase.

MICHAEL WEBER

CONFESSIONS
OF AN INTERNET AUCTION JUNKIE

HOW TO SELL VIRTUALLY ANYTHING ON THE INTERNET

CD-ROM INCLUDED

PRIMA TECH

A Division of Prima Publishing

A Division of Prima Publishing

Prima Publishing and colophon are registered trademarks of Prima Communications, Inc. PRIMA TECH is a trademark of Prima Communications, Inc., Roseville, California 95661.

Kit-Cat Clock is a registered trademark of the California Clock Co; AOLpress is a registered trademark of America Online, Inc; Microsoft, FrontPage, Internet Explorer, Office Pro, Notepad, Outlook, Windows, and Word are trademarks or registered trademarks of Microsoft Corporation in the United States and other countries. Netscape is a registered trademark of Netscape Communications Corporation in the United States and other countries. Corel and WordPerfect are registered trademarks of Corel Corporation or Corel Corporation Limited in Canada, the United States and/or other countires. Jasc is a registered trademark and PaintShop Pro is a trademark of Jasc Software, Inc.

Important: Prima Publishing cannot provide software support. Please contact the appropriate software manufacturer's technical support line or Web site for assistance.

Prima Publishing and the author have attempted throughout this book to distinguish proprietary trademarks from descriptive terms by following the capitalization style used by the manufacturer.

Information contained in this book has been obtained by Prima Publishing from sources believed to be reliable. However, because of the possibility of human or mechanical error by our sources, Prima Publishing, or others, the Publisher does not guarantee the accuracy, adequacy, or completeness of any information and is not responsible for any errors or omissions or the results obtained from use of such information. Readers should be particularly aware of the fact that the Internet is an ever-changing entity. Some facts may have changed since this book went to press.

Library of Congress Catalog Card Number: 00-10733

ISBN: 0-7615-3085-1

00 01 02 03 04 HH 10 9 8 7 6 5 4 3 2 1

Printed in the United States of America

In memory of
Arthur Weber, my father, who taught
me the value of wholesale.

Dedicated to
Selma Slater, my mother, who
taught me the value of retail.

Acknowledgments

This book was written and published in less than nine months but it's not a quickie book. Research was complete the day writing began and I had a marvelous machine behind me, Prima Tech Publishing. I want to thank them for moving mountains, and for their agility and support.

This book is a collaborative effort in which an army of people contributed. I'd especially like to thank my publisher, Stacy Hiquet, and editor, Estelle Manticas, in addition to the legion of other artists and editors at Prima who worked on this book behind the scenes. I want to thank my agents, Joel Gotler of Artist's Management Group and Noah Lukeman of Lukeman Literary Management, for their steadfast enthusiasm and for delivering on their promise to get me a book deal between Thanksgiving and Christmas.

Last but not least I'd like to thank my family and friends; Rick Weber, Paul Ropp, Nicole Kiviat, Jamila Jones, Buddy my Lhasa Apso, and Linda Eastman for being an angel.

About the Author

Before pursuing a career in Hollywood as a screenwriter, Michael Weber produced over $35 million in television commercials for America's premiere advertising agencies and their clients on Madison Avenue. He is the recipient of five Clio Awards. As Executive Producer for top production companies, Mr. Weber developed and led a seminar for The Learning Annex entitled "How To Produce Television Commercials." He is a founding member of the Association Of Independent Commercial Producers, the AICP, and was integral in establishing the organization's presence on the West Coast.

Mr. Weber has worked for several Hollywood studios, including Columbia Pictures and MGM, and has written 14 screenplays. He became a computer fanatic when he started budgeting films and television commercials on an IBM 8086. In 1998 he launched Zenweb Creative Services, an Internet advertising agency, and began developing a retail Web site. His travels soon led to eBay, where Mr. Weber got hooked on Internet auctions.

Contents at a Glance

Contents

Chapter 3
Selling: Secrets of a Master Marketeer 27

Chapter 4
Feedback: You're Only as Good as Your
Reputation. 39

Chapter 5
Navigation and Negotiation: Are Dutch
Auctions Held in Holland? 53

Part II
Experimentation: Closet Mining 63

Chapter 6
Nothing Could Be Finer Than to Be a
Closet Miner 65

Chapter 7
A Crash Course in Technobabble:
Why ASCII? 77

Chapter 8
Great Advertising Equals Great Auctions:
Let's Light This Candle!. 107

Chapter 9
Surviving the Digital Blitzkrieg: Switching
Hats and Selling Kit-Cats 121

Chapter 17
Finding Your Own Niche: Fishing Around 205

Chapter 18
The Web Is Your Oyster: Open a Web Site
and They Will Click! 215

Chapter 19
The Merchant of Visa: The Buck Stops Here . . . 231

Chapter 20
The Eighth Continent: The State Of
Cyberspace 239

Index. 245

How to Sell a 50-Pound Doorstop

A man turned on his printer one day and it whined, wheezed, and died in an acrid puff of smoke. A message appeared on the computer monitor: FATAL ERROR — SERVICE PRINTER IMMEDIATELY! The situation grew even bleaker at The Service Center, a local computer store. A technician informed him that his printer would take three weeks to fix and would cost $400. "Four hundred bucks," the man muttered, "I could buy a new printer that prints twice as fast for less than that!"

Al, the salesman, chimed in on cue: "You're right! This beauty over here was awarded best printer by *PC Magazine* and you can take it home today for less than it would cost to fix up that old clunker."

As Al wrote the sale for a new $359 printer, the man tried to bargain. "Tell you what, Al. My old printer cost me almost a grand. Knock off the sales tax and you guys can keep it. I'm sure you can fix it up and sell it for lots of money."

Al laughed. "Face it, pal. That old dinosaur ain't nothing but a 50-pound doorstop!"

Later, as the man hoisted the broken printer over his head to chuck it in a trash bin, a thought occurred: "Freeze! This sucker has a 4MB RAM chip in it and I just replaced the toner cartridge. I might be able to sell those parts on that Internet auction Web site I keep hearing about!" He'd never sold anything on eBay before in his life but figured he'd give it a try. By the time he finished stripping the old printer he had two RAM chips, a toner cartridge, a paper tray, a power cord, a printer cable, the manuals, software, and some assorted accessories.

He knew nothing about programming HTML or uploading files in order to include photos of the printer parts in the auctions. He simply listed them as plain text "For Sale" ads in eBay's Printer Accessories Category. It cost him $2.25 to list nine separate auctions.

A few days later the man checked back to see how his auctions were doing and his mind was blown! The bidding was hot and heavy. The toner cartridge had skyrocketed past $83 and the 4MB RAM chip, for which he'd paid only $18, was now at $48. Apparently lots of folks wanted his stuff! When the auctions closed and he tallied the bids they added up to $336, just $23 shy of the bill for his new printer. And let's not forget: these parts were from the very same "old dinosaur" that Al, a computer professional, wouldn't give him $30 for a week earlier. At that moment an Internet auction junkie was born!

The story is true. It happened to me.

Profile of an Internet Auction Junkie

My name is Michael and I'm an Internet auction junkie. I sell more Kit-Cat clocks than anyone on eBay. It's a lucrative pastime and oodles of fun but auctioning products on the Internet wasn't my original calling. My career began in advertising; I'd produced $35 million worth of television commercials on Madison Avenue before segueing to Hollywood, where I began screenwriting.

My first studio gig was on the Burbank lot at Columbia Pictures. Back in the good old days, before the PC, we writers depended on a unionized secretarial pool to type our scripts. All of the writers hoarded their favorite typist. My favorite was Joy; I sequestered and inundated her with script changes. When a fellow writer inquired whether I knew of any good typists, I always lied through my teeth and replied no.

Then one day a computer salesman showed me the light. He taught me how to format a screenplay on an Epson computer using WordPerfect 3. It was a transcendental experience that empowered me to sever my shackles to the studio typing pool once and forever. I plunked down $3,500 on my first personal computer and released Joy from indentured servitude.

I was extremely proud of my 12MHz 286 with 4 megabytes of RAM and a 40 megabyte hard disk. It was an exotic speed-demon that came with a new-fangled contraption called a mouse. I've owned every iteration of the x86 processor since. I was a computer junkie long before I became an Internet auction junkie!

Since I was knee-high, my late father, a dress manufacturer, instilled in me the mantra, "Always buy wholesale." I wish he could have been there the day I discovered eBay, the Mother of all Internet Auctions. It was wholesale heaven! The prices were absolutely ridiculous, below wholesale, lower than I'd ever seen. I remember asking myself *who are these people and how can they sell this stuff so cheap?* Where do they get it? Are they making a profit, striking it rich? I was fascinated, hooked; I wanted to be one of them.

I'd toss and turn all night, in the clutches of surreal Internet auction nightmares. I whiled away days that turned into weeks studying them, browsing the auction sites, looking for a hint, a sign, a bolt of lighting. Then, one night a revelation hit. I had a bonanza of valuable property that I had no use for! My collection of cigarette lighters, for example—I'd quit smoking twelve years before! Then there was my camera collection. I'd collected so many cameras over the years that I could barely remember some of them.

What else was in that closet? I hopped out of bed at four in the morning, flung open the closet door, and saw gold! Golf clubs, stereo equipment, computer peripherals, software, books, tapes, my old pool cue, a Vega-matic; my closet was a gold mine and I was going to mine it!

You're no different from me. Regardless of who you are, whatever your station in life, you have merchandise other people want and will gladly pay for—hundreds, perhaps thousands of dollars worth of stuff you've stopped using and have long since forgotten! Internet auctions have not only leveled the selling playing field, they've stolen the ball and moved the game to a new arena. Never before in the history of mankind has it been easier to sell merchandise. Simply put, Internet auctions provide a new sales outlet for people who never had one before, people like us!

The Buying/Selling Equation

The acts of buying and selling are inexorably linked, like inhaling and exhaling are to breathing. Inhale and you make money, exhale and you spend it. An effective seller is by definition a savvy shopper, and wise shoppers by definition make the most successful sellers. The four sections of this book examine buying and selling in incrementally greater detail. Because it's far more difficult to earn money than spend it, the book places more emphasis on selling than buying. The objective is to teach you how to integrate both to become a proficient consumer!

> **Part One.** Casual Use: Browsing

> **Part Two.** Experimentation: Closet Mining

> **Part Three.** Addiction: The Closet Mining Crossroads

> **Part Four.** Recovery: For Professionals Only

There's an old adage about dogs and children that applies to this book, too: "You'll get as much out of it as you put into it." Participate and you'll profit, learn and you will earn! You can put the book down after Part I and have a reasonably sophisticated overview of Internet auctions. But the real fun begins with Part II, Experimentation. As the profits roll in from mining your closet you'll get a taste of what it's like to be an Internet auctioneer.

Unfortunately, all closet miners arrive at the same crossroads. They run out of stuff to sell! Two paths face you. Down one you'll quit Internet auctions cold turkey, down the other you'll become a professional Internet auctioneer. Part III, Addiction, coaches how to avoid common mistakes while replenishing your depleted inventory. Recovery, Part IV, transforms your auctions into commercials for your Web site and provides customers access through a private portal. You can derive an income selling products on the Internet. The question is do you have what it takes to become a garage millionaire?

Internet auctions are an outgrowth of the Internet itself. To master them you must grasp the fundamentals of several related disciplines:

> FTP Internet

> HTML Programming

> Graphics and Design

> Buying

> Selling

> Advertising and Marketing

> E-Commerce

> Self Employment

Many books have been dedicated to each subject. This book bridges the gap by placing under a single cover just what you need to know about each in order to master Internet auctions. Reading is only the starting point. To get the most out of this book you must regularly put it down and complete the assignments at the end of the chapter. Good luck and have a blast!

Ideas Are Like Radio Waves

Did you ever read a book or see a movie and think, "*I once had an idea just like that*"? I learned a secret a long time ago that I believe is the key to creativity: The greatest ideas in the world are free, out there like radio waves. But your radio must be turned on and tuned into the proper channel to receive them. This book challenges you to be creative, as the same idea pool available to the best writers, designers, photographers, and artists is also available to you. Your Internet auctions are nothing more than an extension of your ideas. Turn on your radio and tune in to the proper channel!

Confessions Conventions

Following are some of the assumptions inherent this book about the equipment you will be using.

- ➤ **Computer**. This book assumes you have access to a computer and know how to use it.
- ➤ **Internet**. This book assumes you have an Internet Service Provider and an e-mail account.
- ➤ **Mouse**. This book assumes that you know how to use a mouse and that you're right-handed. Right-click means right-click unless you're left-handed like me and have rearranged your mouse accordingly. Lefties should *left-click* instead.
- ➤ **CD-ROM Drive.** The entire book is on the CD-ROM, in addition to hyperlinks, software, and tools to assist in the creation of successful Internet auctions. The hyperlinks referred to in each chapter are located on the CD-ROM as well. Obviously you must have a CD-ROM drive to take advantage of this invaluable tool.

NOTE

While not technically an assumption, what you should also know about this book is that it's about Internet auctions in general, not just eBay. But because eBay has the biggest database and user base, and is the largest repository of intrinsic values, you'll be taught how to tap these invaluable resources in particular.

Confessions is not just a book. At optimum it's a multimedia experience designed to move you seamlessly from your couch to your computer to the Internet. Experiment with the CD-ROM. You'll soon discover it's far more than a tool or a resource. It's a roller coaster ride on the Internet. Have a good trip!

PART I

Casual Use: Browsing

CHAPTER 1

Reap What You Sow: Money in Your Mailbox

➤ **A Brief Overview of Online Auctions**

➤ **What is an Internet Auction?
A Web Site within a Web Site!**

➤ **Assignment 1: Browse and Register**

√

Some people are addicted to computers and surfing the Web, others to shopping or auctions. I'm addicted to money in my mailbox! I receive so many checks in the mail each day that I had to buy an electric letter opener.

Internet auctions are a lot like farming—grubby work at first. But if you plant your seeds right (that is, feature catchy auction ads for good niche products) you'll reap a bountiful harvest. You can then lean back on your porch in a rocking chair, sip a mint julep, and watch your greenbacks grow.

Kit-Cat clocks like the one in Figure 1.1 are my cash crop. I grow Classic black and white models over yonder and chrome Millennium Editions over here; those French lilac and Seafoam green 1999 Limited Editions in the next field will soon be rotated with 2000's colors. In the barn just beyond, the clocks are hand-jeweled with glimmering Austrian crystals.

Once or twice a week I harvest as many clocks as are necessary to fulfill my Internet auction orders. Depending on the week, I net anywhere from $75 to $150 an hour auctioning Kit-Cat clocks. But it's grueling work. I must sow my seeds (that is, list my auctions) religiously, sift through torrents of e-mail, maintain a database of form letter responses, communicate with my customers in an expedient manner, promptly digitize customer orders and personal data; create invoices, purchase orders, and mailing labels, and ship customers their products within a given window of expectation.

Figure 1.1 *My cash crop is Kit-Cat Clocks*

On top of all this, frequent trips to the bank and post office are required, and tedious chores like bookkeeping and HTML programming constantly loom.

That's Internet auctions for you in a nutshell: the good, the bad, and the ugly! But fear not. This book's mission is to explain the arcane and make palatable the mundane.

A Brief Overview of Online Auctions

Auctions predate most other forms of entertainment and are one of the earliest forms of commerce. Before books, theater, movies, radio, television, computers, and the Internet, there were auctions. Auctions are a perfect example of democracy in the marketplace, as every item in an auction has a *natural* value. Fads come and go but auctions have survived for two basic reasons: they work, and they're fun. Internet auctions are the latest metamorphosis.

Nobody could have envisioned what Internet auctions would become back in 1995. Not even Pierre Omidyar, who launched eBay on a balmy Labor Day afternoon a few weeks after Microsoft's release of Windows 95. The stars must have really been aligned in the heavens on that cusp, because these two products, one by David and the other by Goliath, were destined to become cornerstones of the Internet.

Omidyar was a computer programmer from Silicon Valley (which may go without saying). His fiancée, an avid Pez collector, kept telling him, "Pierre, I need a place to swap my Pez dispensers on the Internet." A flashbulb popped in Pierre's head and eBay was born. Not only did it immediately fill the Pez dispenser void by creating a Web site where collectors could get together and trade their wares, but eBay went on to become the world's first Internet auction site—a place where ordinary folks could buy and sell their stuff. In September of 1998 eBay went public at $15 a share. Six months later, in April 1999, the stock hit $240 a share, a whopping 1600 percent appreciation! Figure 1.2 gives you the picture—including what happened next.

The hallmark of most Internet businesses is that they don't turn a profit. eBay turned a profit in its first quarter. Wall Street loves a winner and Internet auctions became a hot business model for a simple reason—they make money! Amazon.com hasn't yet broken even, but its auction site has. See, Internet auctions get you coming and going; every time an item sells they take a cut, and most charge to list items as well.

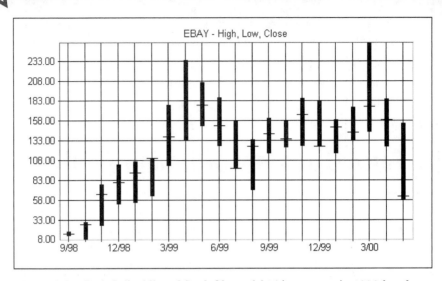

Figure 1.2 *eBay's Split Adjusted Stock Chart. A $15 investment in 1998 bought a heck of a roller-coaster ride!*

When I began tracking Internet auctions in early 1999, eBay had 1.5 million items for sale in 1,000 categories, and 600 million page views per month. By the summer of 2000, it had 4 million items in over 4,300 categories with 1.6 *billion* page views per month. eBay's capacity has quadrupled in only 18 months, despite mounting competition.

eBay is the 800-pound gorilla of the Internet auction business—but a rumble in the jungle is inevitable. Fairmarket is a new alliance of auction heavyweights including Microsoft, Lycos, Tripod, Xoom, ZDNET, PBS, CBS Sportsline, Dell, Excite, CompUSA, Cyberian Outpost, Newline Cinema, and VH1. They've pledged a substantial war chest to wrest market share from eBay. Yahoo and Amazon are already nipping at eBay's heels with auctions of their own. If you added up all of the auction sites on the Internet, big and small, you'd count over 800. All because Pierre Omidyar's fiancée needed a place to swap her Pez dispensers!

At this moment in time, other Internet auction sites pale in comparison to eBay. Yahoo, the second largest, doesn't advertise statistics so I took the liberty of adding them up. They have just under a million items listed for auction compared to eBay's 4 million. In the all-important "page hits per month" comparison no one approaches eBay's staggering 1.6 billion.

eBay's biggest ace in the hole may be brand loyalty and name recognition. David Letterman and Jay Leno have cracked so many jokes about the site that eBay has become ingrained in the lexicon of American water-cooler culture. Who hasn't heard of eBay? It is the first, the biggest, and the most professionally run auction site. In addition, it attracts the most reliable buyers and has made lots of investors rich.

What is an Internet Auction? A Web Site within a Web Site!

The Internet is populated by millions of Web sites that almost nobody visits. *Destination portals*, on the other hand, are Web sites that are visited regularly by millions of people. An Internet auction is a Web site within a destination portal, such as Amazon, eBay, or Yahoo. The express purpose is to get millions of people to pass by your virtual storefront (your Internet auction ad). Internet auctions provide a sales outlet for those who never had one before.

How I Got Hooked on Buying

I was casually browsing eBay one fateful afternoon a few weeks after my printer parts sold, and I couldn't believe my eyes! MS Office Pro, Microsoft's $350 flagship product, was selling for 25 bucks.

Hundreds of vendors were hawking thousands of copies so it wasn't an aberration. I consider myself a shrewd consumer and something stunk. The day before, my three favorite shopping bots had scoured the Internet to ferret out the best price on MS Office, and all three zeroed in on Onsale.com for $239 with free shipping. (More on shopping bots in Chapter 2.) I had ordered it, confident I'd found the best deal. Now I felt duped! My blood boiled; I swore I'd get to the bottom of it. In the sea of headlines, one auction ad stood out: WHERE TO BUY MICROSOFT OFFICE PRO FOR $17.

I clicked on it and read:

> For the price of a Happy Meal I'll provide you with the most closely guarded secret on the Internet—where to find Microsoft Office Pro for just $17.00 or less! You can easily earn hundreds of dollars per auction, thousands of dollars a week, selling just this one product, Microsoft Office Pro.

It was my first Internet auction bid and I wasn't alone; hundreds of people had bid on this item before me. The item in question was simply a link to a list of distributors who sold MS Office for $17 in quantity. The auctioneer was raking in eight bucks a copy for information that cost him nothing—that's quite a markup! My second bid came moments later in an auction for MS Office Pro. I paid $23 for an original equipment manufacturers (OEM) copy and promptly canceled the retail version I'd ordered the day before for $239. The printer parts bonanza and bargain basement software planted the seeds of addiction. I didn't realize it that day but I was getting hooked on Internet auctions.

NOTE

Dutch auctions for OEM software were commonplace in 1999. As you can see in Figure 1.3, more copies of MS Office Pro were auctioned than any other title. It was a phenomenon! Hundred of sellers earned a living auctioning just this single product.

This book does not advocate the use of illegitimate software, under any circumstance. On the contrary, it warns against illegal software use several times throughout. My goal is not merely to teach what to do, but also what to avoid.

How about you? Would you like to regain precious living space and earn some extra money? Internet auctions are the greatest boon to spring cleaning since the advent of the garage sale. If you find the idea of money in your mailbox appealing, read on. But be forewarned: Internet auctions are addicting!

Assignment 1: Browse and Register

Time to get your feet wet. Wade along the shore awhile. You don't have to dive right in. Browse the auction sites to your heart's content, but before you can bid on or sell anything you'll have to take the plunge and register—it only takes a few minutes. In addition to a computer with a modem and an ISP account you'll need an e-mail address and credit card (in most cases) to register. Devise a short, descriptive user name that's easy to type and remember. Use the same or a similar user name and password on each auction site.

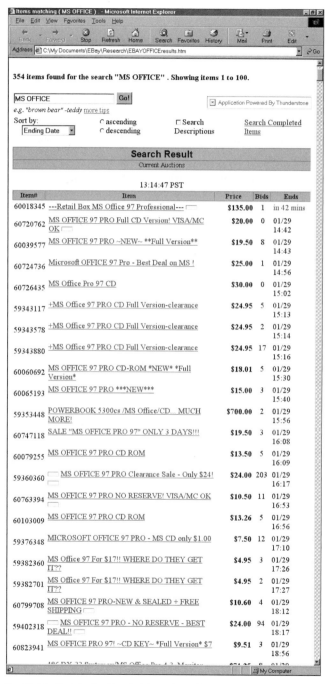

Figure 1.3 *354 individual sellers held auctions for thousands of copies of MS Office Pro on eBay on January 21, 1999. This occurred every day for almost a year on every major auction site.*

Then do the following:

1. Insert the *Confessions* CD-ROM disk into your computer's CD-ROM drive.

2. Open confess.htm.

3. Click Internet Auction Sites under Links in your Web browser's right frame.

4. Click the register link under Amazon, eBay, and Yahoo, and register with each auction site.

5. Check out over 800 other auction sites by clicking the Goto.com banner.

CHAPTER 2

Buying:
Secrets of a
Master Bidder

The Internet has changed the way people interact. It should therefore come as no surprise that Internet auctions have changed the way people transact business with one another. No other realm of commerce relies on blind faith and the honor system the way Internet auctions do. What's the allure? What sets Internet auctions apart?

> **Bargains**. Products may be priced at pennies on the dollar.

> **Unique and exotic merchandise**. Hard-to-find items suddenly seem almost common.

> **Rural and foreign merchandise**. Products that buyers can't purchase locally are right at hand.

> **Enjoyment**. Internet auctions are a hybrid pastime, a cross between shopping, surfing the Web, and gambling.

> **Profit**. Auctions are a bona fide form of e-commerce and one of the most profitable.

Buyers are at a distinct disadvantage in an Internet auction. Like the odds in Vegas, which always favor the house, Internet auctions favor the seller. Why? Because sellers are an Internet auction's cash cow. Without them there would be no buyers. Remember, it costs nothing to bid on an item but usually costs something to list it. Here's how the deck is stacked:

> **Buyers never get to feel or test-drive the merchandise**. They must rely on the seller's description and photo.

> **Buyers never get to look a seller in the eyes**. There's only an implied assumption of honesty. Auction site feedback works, but it is not infallible. I'm told that the two burglars from New England who were recently busted for auctioning $30,000 worth of stolen booty on eBay both had excellent feedback ratings!

> **Buyers must wait for an auction to close**. There's no instant gratification.

> **Buyers have to live with a seven- to ten-day lag time**. That's how long it typically takes for sellers to receive payment and ship the item, and for it to be delivered.

> **Buyers must pay for merchandise up front.** Many sellers don't accept credit cards, leaving buyers financially exposed.

> **Buyers are stuck with the merchandise.** All sales are final. Internet auction bids are binding contracts so there's no recourse to return an item. eBay backs each auction with $200 fraud insurance, but the $25 deductible often exceeds the sale price.

The Five Commandments of Master Bidding

Once you understand that the deck is stacked there are several things you can do to protect yourself. These suggestions rely on using common sense and obeying one's own instincts.

First Commandment: Do Not Suspend Your Disbelief

Internet auctions defy logic and common sense. Where else but in an Internet auction would somebody stuff $30, $40, or $50 cash in an envelope, put a 33–cent stamp on it, and send it to the P.O. box of somebody he doesn't even know? I've been paid in that manner dozens of times. In the movie business this phenomenon is called *suspension of disbelief*. Don't do it! My advice is to never pay in cash and always pay by credit card if the option is available.

A recent auction on eBay, widely covered by the news media, provides a good object lesson on suspension of disbelief. Following is an excerpt written by Andrew Quinn for Reuters:

> The man who sparked an art world controversy by accepting a $135,805 bid for a painting he allegedly found at a garage sale was suspended by the online auction company eBay Wednesday for seeking to secretly boost the sales price. Sacramento lawyer Ken Walton, who listed the painting under the name "Golfpoorly," had used a different alias to place a $4,500 bid on his own lot, a practice known as "shilling" aimed at prompting bidding wars among other participants, eBay said. The green and orange painting eventually drew three bids of more than $135,000 before attracting a top bid of $135,805.

eBay said that it later had found that one of the some 95 bids on the painting had been placed by Walton himself using an alias user name.

The painting, advertised as a "great big wild abstract art painting," bore some resemblance to works produced in the 1950's by Diebenkorn, one of California's best known artists. Diebenkorn paintings have sold for well over $1 million in recent sales. Walton made no reference to Diebenkorn in his description of the work. But he did include a number of hints—including a close-up photo of a hole in the canvas near a Diebenkorn-style "RD" signature—which helped to prompt the furious bidding. He also said he had purchased the work at a garage sale in Berkeley, where Diebenkorn had worked in the 1950s.

Walton's tale began to unravel late Tuesday when he admitted "making up" elements of his story about the painting, including the allegation that the hole in the canvas had been caused by his child's tricycle. He is, in fact, single. Kevin Pursglove, an eBay spokesman, said the company had found evidence of one "shill" bid in the auction, and that such bids are almost always placed by sellers seeking to inflate the price of their offerings. "Shilling is one of the biggest concerns that our users have because it gets to the very integrity of the bidding process," Pursglove said. "When we hear about it, we move very fast."

Colleen Valles of The Associated Press did some additional digging. Her report was filed in the middle of May 2000.

Walton has sold 33 paintings on eBay since March 30. He was threatened with a lawsuit last summer when he offered a work signed "P. Gray." The buyer, Nebraska businessman Michael Luther, thought the painting was done by California artist Henry Percy Gray. He paid $7,600 for what ended up being an amateur's work with a recently added signature. Walton denied adding the signature.

In his latest eBay offering, Walton did not say who did the painting, only that he had kept it in his garage. A photograph of the painting showed the signature "RD," the way Diebenkorn typically signed his work. Art experts said the photo displayed on eBay shows some of the abstract expressionism techniques that Diebenkorn used in 1952. Diebenkorn, who died in 1993, switched styles twice, but spent his last 25 years painting mostly lines and geometric forms in the brilliant colors that had become his trademark.

To the 94 suckers who bid on this turkey, besides the shill himself, I have the following message: *Do due diligence and do not suspend your disbelief!*

Second Commandment: Feel the Force

This is what I call the precautionary commandment. On the Internet, one never knows who's clicking the mouse on the other end of the line. Mixed in among the wonderful people you'll encounter on the World Wide Web is a new breed of menace: people who—for whatever reason—are not what they claim.

The Internet is the ultimate democracy because of its anonymity. All men, women, and scam artists are created equal. I'm not trying to make you paranoid but I want you to keep your antenna up. *Obey your instincts at all times!*

Third Commandment: Follow the Feedback

A buyer or seller's *feedback rating* is the number next to his or her name (see Figure 2.1). "Zenweb" is my eBay user name. I'm proud of my feedback rating of 237 Positives and 0 Negatives; by the time you read this it'll hopefully be higher!

Clicking on the rating number links you to a page of comments about that buyer or seller posted by people who have already concluded transactions with him. Checking seller feedback should be a regular part of your bidding routine because doing so—and then only bidding in auctions by sellers with good feedback—increases your odds of not getting burnt. A small percentage of neutral or negative feedback on a seller or buyer is acceptable. Bear in mind, there are people in this world who have unrealistic expectations. eBay recently overhauled its feedback system to address this fact, allowing sellers to respond to vindictive and injurious feedback. Chapter 5 explores feedback in more depth, but suffice it to say, *beware of sellers with a high percentage of negative feedback!*

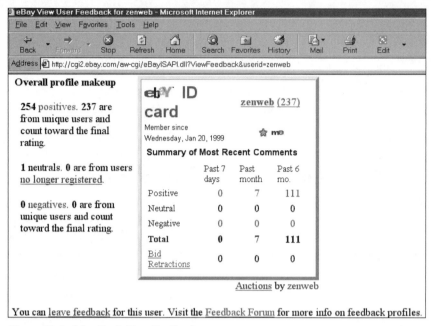

Figure 2.1 *My eBay's User Feedback page*

Fourth Commandment: Always Use a Shopping Bot

A shopping what? *Bot* is short for robot. Shopping bots are dedicated software agents that perform Internet-specific tasks such as ferreting out the best price and availability on a product (see Figure 2.2). In essence they are glorified search engines. You don't really need to know how bots work, you simply need to know how to use them. That's their beauty.

Suppose you're in the market for a new color inkjet printer. You can query a bot in a variety of ways.

> ➤ **By category**. Type **color inkjet printer** in the bot's search box. The bot displays every available color inkjet printer broken down by manufacturer, model number, and price.

> ➤ **By specific product**. Most bots supply product reviews, but there's good buzz on the Epson Stylus 900, so let's search for the best price on that. The bot turns up a screen like the one in Figure 2.3, listing every merchant who carries the Stylus 900, broken down by price, shipping fee, and number of units in stock.

Figure 2.2 *CNET's Shopper.com is my favorite shopping bot.*

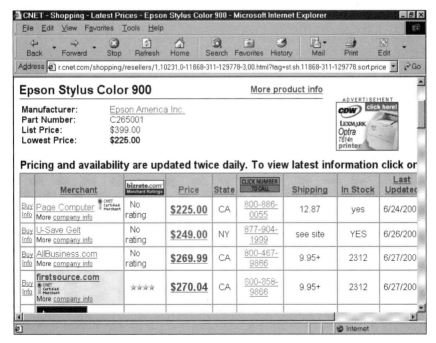

Figure 2.3 *A shopping bot query for the Epson 900 sorted by price*

As you can see, Page Computer squished the competition at $225, but when I clicked on their site I discovered the printer was a refurb. The next-lowest price, $249 at U-Save Gelt, not only applied to a brand new printer, but the seller also threw in a $50 manufacturer's rebate from Epson, bringing the bottom line down to $199. On this particular day, U-Save Gelt lived up to its name. Check out the price tags for a Stylus 900 at the bottom of the page shown in Figure 2.4.

> **By type of product.** What good is an inkjet printer without inkjet paper? Type **inkjet paper** in the bot's search box and choose Epson Photo inkjet paper because they manufactured the printer; you should get results like those in Figure 2.5.

Who says the best things in life aren't free? Shopping bots are one of the Internet's greatest miracles. I recommend using three bots for each query because your results may vary from bot to bot and search to search. Certain bots are product specific, such as digitalcamera.com for digital cameras. Pricewatch.com and Goto.com both provide auction-specific bots that query hundreds of auction sites. Links to Pricewatch and Goto can be found under Services on the *Confessions* CD-ROM.

Buy Info	pcWonders.com More company info	★★★★★	**$349.00**	NJ	800-753-9363	11.96+	yes	6/26/200
Buy Info	BuyMoreProducts More company info	★★★★	**$349.00**	CA	800-997-4990	4.25+	Yes	6/22/200
Buy Info	Outpost.com More company info	★★★★★	**$349.95**	CT	800-856-9800	FREE OVERNIGHT	Instock	6/26/200
Buy Info	PCZone *In Business Since 1986* More company info	★★★★	**$349.99**	WA	888-246-3306	5.49+	IN STOCK	6/27/200
Buy Info	ComputAbility More company info	No rating	**$349.99**	WI	800-554-2184	Starts at $5.50	Yes	6/27/200
Buy Info	PC Mall More company info	★★★★	**$349.99**	CA	888-932-8610	Starts at $5.50	Yes	6/27/200
Buy Info	Digital Distributors More company info	No rating	**$399.00**	NY	800-943-2000	see site	YES	6/22/200

Re-sort By Price / Sponsor

Figure 2.4 *Without due diligence it would be easy to pay a couple of hundred bucks more!*

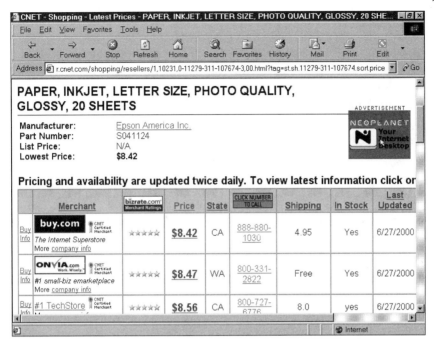

Figure 2.5 *You can determine the lowest price on practically anything with the right shopping bot.*

In this day and age it's crazy to pay full price. Being a savvy consumer used to be an arduous task, but thanks to the Internet, it's now child's play. Simply go to your three favorite shopping bots, key in the model number of the product you desire, and sit back while the bots scour the Internet for the lowest price. If you don't have three favorite shopping bots click Shopping Bots on the *Confessions* CD-ROM and use the first three. Now, repeat after me: *Always buy wholesale!*

Playing The Burn Rate

Would you like to know one of the Internet's dirtiest little secrets? A lot of Web sites that lure you with ridiculously low prices are selling the merchandise at below their wholesale cost—they're losing money on every sale. What would perpetuate such madness?

Wall Street, in its wisdom, measures the upside potential of an e-tail venture by gross sales, not the bottom line. Amazon.com has lost money every quarter by selling books below cost, only to see its stock price climb higher. The stock analysts even have a name for this new millennium Ponzi scheme: the *Burn Rate*. I can't explain the economics of it, but I do suggest that you play the Burn Rate whenever you make a purchase; it's the best way I know to save big bucks. Question: What's the best way to play the Burn Rate? Answer: *Use shopping bots!*

Fifth Commandment: Never Bid on an Item You Can Buy for the Same Price or Less

If you can buy an item outright for the same price or less, then why bid on it? As previously mentioned, e-tailers provide greater consumer protection than do Internet auction sites. For your own peace of mind it's imperative to ascertain a product's inherent worth before plunking down your hard-earned dollars. Do research, also known as *due diligence*. That's the trick behind being a Master Bidder.

Finding What You Want on an Auction Site

An auction site is not unlike a shopping bot. They're the Yin and Yang of the savvy Web consumer, master one and you've mastered the other. The two means by which you can locate what you're looking for on an auction site are *searching* and *browsing*.

Searching

Searching is synonymous with the Internet. Like the key that ignites the engine in a car, the Internet would have gone nowhere without a way to search it. Before there was a graphical World Wide Web, the Internet was an incongruous network of mainframe computers on college campuses and military installations used by academics to query one another. The technology that enables computers to search for and share information with each other was and is the Internet's raison d'etre.

Yahoo! the granddaddy of all Internet portals, was and is a search engine. Amazon is a glorified search engine, too—without that capability it couldn't sell books. eBay is also a search engine, but in my opinion it stands apart. eBay is the largest repository of intrinsic value in the universe! You'll learn how to tap this resource and discover numerous other search techniques over the course of this book.

Here's an example: Suppose you were in the market for some sports memorabilia autographed by Mark McGuire; you'd type **Mark McGuire autographed** in the search box and be linked to every item on the auction site autographed by Mark McGuire (see Figure 2.6). Be sure to check Search Item and Description.

The difference between a shopping bot and an auction site is that an auction site is an internal database—a Web site within a Web site—whereas a shopping bot is an external database that gathers data from other Web sites. To end users they work the same way, however.

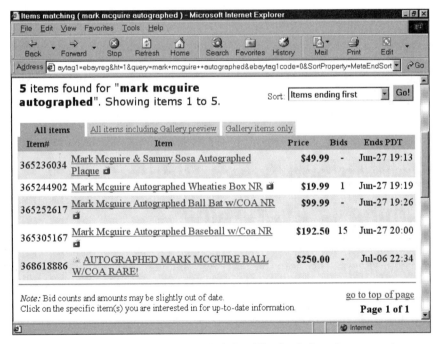

Figure 2.6 *Mark McGuire memorabilia is hot. The day before, there were nine auctions.*

Master Search

Auction services like Pricewatch.com and Goto.com search multiple Internet auctions for a particular item. Shopping bots like CNET do the same in the B2C marketplace. A simple search on some of these sites before you bid or buy can literally save you thousands of dollars over time! Pricewatch.com and Goto.com can be found on the *Confessions* CD-ROM under Services. You'll find CNET's Shopper.com link under Shopping Bots.

Browsing

I cut my Internet auction teeth on browsing. My hard drive is still littered with hundreds of HTML downloads dating back to day one. Internet auction site maps, tutorials, featured auctions, hot auctions, auctions featured by category, category overviews, rules and regulations, HTML and photo how-to's, fees—without all these files and documents I could never have written this book!

When I first discovered Internet auctions they were so exotic and foreign that I became confused about how to proceed. Browsing was the solution to my confusion. Downloading files and studying them offline for hours on end gave me the lay of the land. Browsing provided an overview, put Internet auctions in context, and distinguished what worked from what didn't. In the coming pages I recommend you do the same. You'll be provided with specific assignments to help get you started.

Sniping and Proxy Bidding— Timing Is Everything

No discussion of bidding would be complete without an examination of proxy bidding and its notorious alter ego, sniping. Internet auctions are a temporal medium—they evolve over time. When you place a simple bid it is but one fleeting moment in the history of that auction. Sniping and proxy bidding are both techniques that take advantage of timing.

Sniping

4:36 a.m. An alarm clock rings. The sniper wakes and rises quickly from her bed. She collects Hermes handkerchiefs, and an auction for a rare one is closing in less than five minutes. She dashes in the dark to her waiting computer and logs on to the auction site. Seven bids for the handkerchief top out at $46.73—what a steal. No new bids since she went to bed, either. This Hermes may be a sleeper, she thinks to herself as she rubs the sleep from her eyes. Three minutes to go and counting. She nonchalantly twists the cap off a Perrier bottle and has a sip. Two minutes to go. Suddenly, a new bid appears for $48.73, the $2 minimum. She knew this was too good to be true—there's another sniper lurking out there somewhere, just as she suspected! But she has the advantage. She knows it takes an average of 32 seconds for a bid to go through. She's been here and done that. She fills out a bid for $50.73 and places it well into the last minute. The seconds tick down toward the end of the auction. 10, 9, 8, 7…. Her winning bid of $50.73 registers with five seconds to go. She screams, "Gotcha sucker!"

You can theoretically beat out a hundred other bidders by a single penny, by sniping. Sniping is timing your bid until the last moment to sandbag your competition and make off with the goods at the lowest price.

"When should I bid and how much?" is the first question you should ask yourself when you find an item you'd like to bid on. If you place a lowball bid early on in the auction, more people will be drawn to that auction. When you bid you validate the item and invite scrutiny and competition. But if you wait until the end of the auction to bid, people may see a goose egg, a big fat zero, next to the number of bids, and they may be less inclined to bid on the items themselves. People covet what other people desire, and vice versa; that's human nature. Sniping takes advantage of this psychology.

When you start running your own auctions you'll discover that a majority of bids come toward the end of the auction. There are two reasons for this: sniping and instant gratification! Bidders snipe because it works, unless of course there's another sniper lurking—*that* can lead to a sniping war.

Sniping is controversial, but I don't understand why. It isn't immoral, illegal, or unfair. Perhaps it's because it takes so many novice bidders by surprise. As an antidote to sniping the three major auction sites recommend proxy bidding (explained below), as do I. Yahoo! and Amazon also give you the option to automatically extend the close of an auction by five or ten minutes, until bid cessation. On eBay, an auction's close time is written in stone.

To snipe or not to snipe? I think it all boils down to personality. To many, sniping is the most enjoyable part of bidding. There are dozens if not hundreds of software programs (mostly available on auction sites) specifically designed to aid and abet sniping.

Personally, I don't snipe. This isn't a value judgment, I'm simply too lazy. I also happen to believe that searching, shopping bots, and proxy bidding are far more effective buying and bidding techniques.

Proxy Bidding

Imagine the previous sniper story with a slightly different ending.... Three minutes to go and counting. She nonchalantly twists the cap off a Perrier bottle and has a sip. Two minutes to go. Nothing! She's surprised. She expected more competition. With little more than a minute to go she places a bid for $48.73, the $2 minimum. But before she can even refresh her Web browser the bid jumps to $50.73. No human could place a bid that fast. Foiled by a proxy bid! She frantically places another bid for $55, the first figure that pops in her head. 5, 4, 3, too late! She loses to a proxy bidder who's probably slumbering out there somewhere, blissfully unaware of her victory.

Proxy bidding is the closest thing to an antidote to sniping. A *proxy bid* is the highest price you're willing to pay, revealed to the public in minimum bid increments. (The amount of the top bid determines the minimum bid increment—the amount a bidder must add to the existing bid to take the lead in the auction.)

Suppose you come across an item you want. There are six bids on it. It opened at $1 and now it's at $17.43, which makes the minimum bid increment $1. You could bid $18.43, but it's likely that others will outbid you. You've crunched the item through some shopping bots and searched the completed auctions results to determine its value, and it is easily worth over $80. What should you do? You have three plays.

> ➤ **Bid $80**. This would scare off most other bidders. You'd probably win but would likely pay too much.

> **Bid $40**. This would separate the men from the boys but you'd still have competition. Others are aware that this item is worth more. You'd only have to come back and bid again.

> **Put in a proxy bid for $80**. This is your best option! I call it the Lazy Man's Snipe. You put in a proxy bid for $80 and now have the winning bid up to $80—but nobody can see what you've done! In this scenario the high bid would now be $18.43. One of your opponents tries to shake off the competition by bidding $40. But your proxy bid immediately raises the high bid to $42, the minimum bid increment of $2 that applies at that price level. Stymied, your opponent raises her bid to $57, the maximum she will pay. Your proxy bid once again raises the high bid, this time to $59. The outcome: your opponent walks away with her tail between her legs, you win the auction with a high bid of $59, and you pocket the $21 difference. You see, you don't have pay the $80 proxy bid amount. You only pay the high bid amount, in this case $59.

Assignment 2: Search and Enjoy

What would you most like to buy right now? Here's how to find the dirt-cheapest available price on that item. Log on to the Internet, start your *Confessions* CD-ROM, and click the CNET Shopper banner under Shopping Bots. Type the model number or brand name in the search box and then select it with your mouse. Copy it to your clipboard and click Search. Get any hits? If not, move on to the next shopping bot, paste the model number or brand name in its search box, and do another search.

Maybe the item you're seeking is exceptionally rare? Click the eBay banner on your *Confessions* CD-ROM under Internet Auction Sites and paste the model number or brand name in eBay's search box. Get any hits? If you did, click the Completed Auctions link to establish that item's intrinsic value. If you received no hits, you're either searching incorrectly, you've entered a typo, or the item you're searching for is too obscure. Repeat the assignment searching for something more mainstream.

Assignment 3: Browse What's Hot

Log on to the Internet, start your *Confessions* CD-ROM, and click the Hot! link below Auctions Sites on eBay. To appear on this page an auction must garner 30 bids or more. Study the headlines and the auctions they lead to. These auctioneers must be doing something right!

Assignment 4: Prepare Your Hard Drive and Web Browser

It's time to prepare your computer and your Web browser for your upcoming Internet auction activities. On your PC, open Windows Explorer. On your Mac, open Finder. Create a new folder on your hard drive and name it Auctions. Create two subdirectories in the Auctions directory and name one Research and the other My Auctions. Now create *bookmark folders* in your Web browser for each Internet auction Web site with which you're registered, naming the folders for the sites—eBay, Amazon, Yahoo! and so on.

Assignment 5: Read eBay's How To Bid Tutorial

For more comprehensive information on bidding, click How To Bid below the eBay banner under Internet Auction Sites on the *Confessions* CD-ROM.

CHAPTER 3

Selling: Secrets of a Master Marketeer

> Scoring a Headline Home Run

> Pricing Your Items Right

> Master Marketeer's Trick of the Trade: Reserve Price Auctions

> Assignment 6: Study What Sells and Why

Some of the most successful Web sites on the Internet were started in garages. Do you have what it takes to become a garage millionaire? Believe it or not, the tools to do so are at your disposal—and you'll learn how to use them in the following pages. This book is as much about thinking as doing. In the end, your Internet auctions are an extension of your ideas. Selling is both an art and a craft; this chapter delves into the art.

One of the best salesmen I have ever seen was a street vendor hawking beads and crystals near Central Park's Sheep Meadow. I watched as he meticulously placed trinkets on a plush velvet blanket. Dappled by the early morning sun, his pebbles suddenly transformed into gems and his hippie beads became fine jewelry.

A procession of Sunday strollers soon began passing by. The street vendor, a young man costumed like a pirate from Penzance, read their faces as they approached and customized his pitch to each with the cadence of a professional auctioneer.

"Rings, bracelets, $5 each. Mix and match, three for $12."

"Latvian quartz, cures headaches, $6."

"Nepalese fertility rings. Two for $16, watch out for twins!"

"Rings, bracelets, mix and match, only $7 apiece."

The spot in front of his blanket turned into Grand Central Station. He was holding court. People crowded around just to see what was going on. As the crowd changed his pitch changed with them. Essentially, he was selling the *same* products to an assorted audience at *different* prices. He was a Master Marketeer!

He sold out by noon: I was in awe. I strolled over to compliment him on his technique as he folded his velvet blanket; he thanked me. I then inquired if he'd ever considered selling his jewelry on the Internet. He grinned sheepishly, and replied, "Nah, where do you think I buy this junk? But I do sell office supplies on eBay." He handed me a Himalayan happiness crystal and walked away, no doubt to tend to his Internet auctions.

Central Park trinket sales and Internet auctions have more in common than you might imagine (see Table 3.1).

Table 3.1 Street Sales vs. Internet Sales

	Street Vendor	Internet Auction
The Bait: an interesting hook.	His pitch, which he altered and experimented with to get people to stop.	Your headline, which you experiment with and alter to get people to click.
The Trap: a virtual store that comes and goes.	His velvet blanket, which transformed his junk into jewels.	Your auction ad, which persuades people to bid on what you're selling.
The Prize: a two-headed dragon!	To the vendor, it's the purchase; to the buyer, a trinket.	To the seller, it's the bid; to the bidder, the win.

Scoring a Headline Home Run

Effective headlines have four characteristics. To score a headline home run, you must touch each of these "bases."

> ➤ **First Base: Conciseness.** Every keystroke and character in a headline counts, literally!
> ➤ **Second Base: Searchable words.** The more searchable words a headline contains, the better.
> ➤ **Third Base: Persuasive pitch.** The goal of a headline is to persuade people to click.
> ➤ **Home Base: Price.** Pricing is the link between your headline and your auction. A great headline topping an incorrectly-priced item is like a pop-up to the outfield.

Writing Concise Headlines

First and foremost, your headline must be concise. eBay allows only 45 characters—including spaces—for a headline. Amazon and Yahoo allow up to 80 keystrokes but they convert capitalized headlines to lowercase; eBay does not.

The first thing you learn on Madison Avenue is to "use limitations and restraints as a creative catalyst." This strategy also applies to Internet auctions. Writing an effective 45-character headline is a formidable challenge, but it can be fun if you approach it as a game and not a burden. When you start closet mining your own treasures you'll get plenty of practice. Here's a few of my Kit-Cat clock headlines. As the numbers in parentheses indicate, all are 45 characters or less.

> JEWELED LIMITED EDITION KIT-CAT CLOCK - RARE! (44)
>
> NEW CHROME KIT-CAT CLOCK MILLENNIUM EDITION! (44)
>
> NEW KIT-CAT PENDULUM CLOCK - ORIGINAL CLASSIC (45)

The best way to count the keystrokes in your headlines is with a word processing program such as Word or WordPerfect. It's advisable to count characters before logging onto an auction site.

NOTE

Numerous differences exist among the major auction sites, and I'll go over them in detail as they come up. You'll notice that eBay refers to *characters* while the others talk *keystrokes*, but that's just a difference in terminology; a character and a keystroke are one and the same.

Writing Searchable Headlines

Most people are too young to remember automats, but they provide a good metaphor for Internet auctions. Figures 3.1 and 3.2 will give you an idea of how the past and present collide.

Automats were popular meeting places, like Internet destination portals are today. As you can see, they were marvels of efficiency and "futuristic" Art Deco design. A vast panorama of windowed, shoebox-sized compartments greeted diners as they entered a large communal dining room. Workers in a hidden kitchen filled each compartment from behind with a plate of fresh chow for which the diners lined up like automatons on an assembly line. The glass doors didn't open—much like a vending machine—until somebody slugged in a nickel, dime, or quarter.

Internet auctions are like cyberspace automats: infinite Internet vending machines. Log on and you are inundated by millions of identical compartments, each containing something different for sale. How do you navigate and find what you're looking for? You could browse: blue plate specials over here, desserts over there—it would be a daunting task. Or you could search. Master Bidders *search*.

Figure 3.1 *Internet auctions are like modern-day automats. Headlines separate the cherry pie from the mashed potatoes.*

Figure 3.2 *Leave your fox fur coat in the closet and wear a bathrobe to the Internet auction. Better yet, auction your fox fur coat!*

Remember the example of the Mark McGuire baseball glove in the last chapter? Place yourself in the buyer's shoes—that's an old Master Marketeer's trick. If Master Bidders search, the best way to lure them to your product—your Internet auction compartment—is to compose a searchable headline.

Five components make a headline searchable. Let's examine the forty-four character headline SWISS GOLD DUNHILL ROLL-A-GAS BUTANE LIGHTER.

> **Manufacturer, make, or brand name.** If an item you're auctioning was commercially manufactured, it most likely has a make and/or brand name. In this case it's "Dunhill."

> **Model or part number.** Many products have both. A model name is generally more searchable than a part number. In the above headline, "Roll-A-Gas" is the model.

> **Description.** What searchable words differentiate your item from others in the same product category? In this case, "Swiss," "gold," and "butane" do.

> **Category.** Auction sites are broken into categories because every product falls into one. The category of the Dunhill is "butane lighter."

> **Hyperbolic buzzwords.** When it comes to headlines, a little hype can go a long way, especially if your hyperbole is searchable. Cap buzzwords and set them off with exclamation points or dollar signs, separated by a keystroke. Above all, be honest. Never misrepresent what you're selling! If these words apply, use them sparingly. The above headline contains no hype.

Common Buzzwords

New	Wholesale
Vintage	Discount
Hot	Save
Rare	Profit
Best	Value
Cherry	Money
Mint	Investment
Top	Rich
Quality	N/R (No Reserve)
Designer	MIB (Merchandise in box)
Collectible	$!

An effective headline need not include all five components, but the best ones do. Is the following forty-four-character headline searchable?

JEWELED LIMITED EDITION KIT-CAT CLOCK - RARE!

The answer is yes. In fact, this headline meets all five criteria:

> **Kit-Cat** is the registered brand name.
> **Jeweled limited edition** is the model.
> **Limited edition** also functions as a description.
> **Clock** is the product category.
> **Rare!** is a hyperbolic buzzword, and the exclamation point conveys excitement!

This headline would wind up on the short-list of anybody searching for a clock, a limited edition, something rare, a Kit-Cat Klock (the actual registered trademark), or a Jeweled Limited Edition Kit-Cat clock, specifically. Notice I took the liberty of changing the brand name Klock to "Clock." Clock is not only the product category, it is tangible. The more you avoid intangibles and non-words such as Klock, the more people will be able to find your auctions. Of course, every rule has exceptions. A Kit-Cat collector might search for "Klock" first. With only 45 characters to work with I was forced to make a choice. I figured more people would ultimately find my auction searching for "Clock" than "Klock."

Writing Persuasive Headlines

There's an old adage in the writing profession: *Writing is rewriting*. Those forty-five characters must add up to a persuasive message that compels others to click (see Table 3.2). As you compose your headline ask yourself, "Would this headline make me click?" Don't list your auction until you answer yes. Work it and rework it, and polish your headline until it shines. Remember, your Internet auctions are extensions of your ideas!

To persuade is to *sway*. I can't teach you the friendly art of persuasion, but you can teach it to yourself. Practice makes perfect, and you'll get plenty. In the meantime, study these persuasive headlines—all of which garnered their auctions thirty bids or more—and count the characters in each. These headlines were collected from eBay's What's Hot page. The numbers in parentheses is the number of bids each headline received.

Table 3.2 Characteristics of Persuasive Headlines

Be:		Don't Be:	
Bold	Dynamic	Cautious	Vague
Clear	Active	Abstract	Passive
Clever	Convincing	Dull	Insulting
Creative	Friendly	Unimaginative	Disrespectful
Honest	Tasteful	Deceitful	Tasteless

- NVIDIA RIVA TNT2 32MB 4X AGP DVD 10 @ $1.00
  (31 Bids)
- SPECKLES BEAR TY EXCLUSIVE E-BEANIE 12 AVAIL
  (41 Bids)
- CALLAWAY BIG BERTHA RH 8 IRON-EXCELLENT!!
  (35 Bids)
- TOKYO MARUI AIRSOFT M9 GBB W/ACCESORIES MIB!!
  (33 Bids)
- PALM IIIE 3E PILOT BY 3COM W/CRADLE *NEW* N/R
  (40 Bids)
- NEW FROM JAPAN! SONY MZ-E800 MINIDISC PLAYER
  (36 Bids)
- NEW!INTEL 566MHZ SYSTEM 64MB,13G,50X,56K,FAST
  (35 Bids)
- AIR JORDAN XV SAMPLE UNRELEASED SLIP-ON MOC
  (44 Bids)
- RAREST 2000 MINT PROOF SET ALL CERTIFIED MS70
  (37 Bids)
- SONY MAVICA MVC FD91 DIGITAL CAMERA BRAND NEW
  (34 Bids)

Pricing Your Items Right

When I was fourteen I bought a watch from a man in Greenwich Village. I was very proud of myself. I'd whittled him down, like my father always told me to do, from $100 to $15. That night at dinner I proudly displayed the watch. As I bragged about my accomplishment, my father's forehead wrinkled and he frowned. He said "I'm disappointed in you, son. You fell for one of the oldest tricks in the book. I wouldn't give you five bucks for that watch." I felt like such an idiot that I wanted to shrivel up and crawl under the table!

After dinner I hopped on a subway and rode back to the Village. I stood on the same street corner, by MacDougal Alley, and started whispering to passers-by, "Psst....wanna buy a watch?" I was determined to double my money. I wanted at least thirty bucks! I didn't realize it until later, but that night was my first auction. The watch glistened in an expensive-looking box, and as I recall it sold rather quickly—for $35! When I told my father the next day, he patted me on the shoulder and said "Good work, son! I hope this taught you a lesson."

"What lesson?" I asked.

"Buy low and sell high!"

Price is not only an ingredient; it is the single most important ingredient of your headline. If your auction isn't priced right, no one will click. You can sell virtually anything if it's priced right. It may be below what you expect—or will accept—and you may even find it insulting, but it's a fundamental law of every auction since time immemorial. Everything has an intrinsic value!

Don't confuse value with cost. One thousand pennies is the same as a $10 bill, right? Well, if you were to auction both on the Internet their value would differ significantly. The pennies would sell for a fraction of their cost whereas the bill would retain most of its value. You can slip a $10 bill in an envelope and mail it for 33 cents. How much does it cost to ship a thousand pennies? According to the Postal Service it would cost $7.50 to send them by Priority Mail. You'd be lucky if somebody bid a buck or two. But somebody *would* bid, and the pennies would sell, because everything has an intrinsic value.

Internet auctions are repositories of the intrinsic value of almost every item known to man. Here's how to tap this wealth of information. Pick an item, any item, and then do a standard Internet auction site search. The example in Figures 3.3 and 3.4 shows a search for prints by the artist Karel Appel, whose work is far more obscure than, say, Picasso's.

You'll be linked to the page of current auctions for Karel Appel prints mixed in among auctions for other items that contain the keyword Appel. The trick is to view the closed auctions linked to this page. Click Search Completed and you'll be whisked to a page that establishes the intrinsic value of recently auctioned Karel Appel prints.

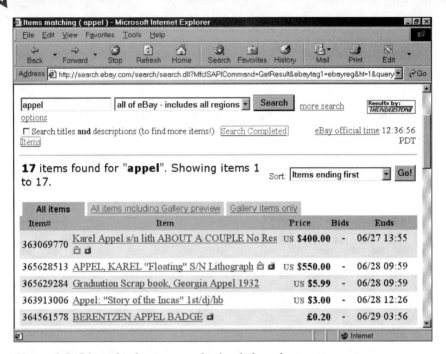

Figure 3.3 *It's not hard to separate the Appels from the oranges.*

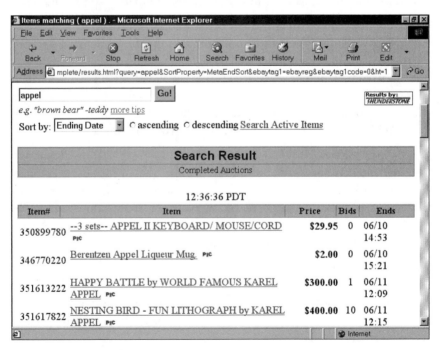

Figure 3.4 *Look at the first auction listed on this page and you'll see why spelling is important when listing your auctions!*

Always determine an item's intrinsic value before listing it. The right item, priced right, is sure to get bids. From the closed auctions on this page I can deduce that Karel Appel prints sell in the $300 to $400 range. I can also infer that the headline NESTING BIRD - FUN LITHOGRAPH by KAREL APPEL was superior to HAPPY BATTLE by WORLD FAMOUS KAREL APPEL because it is far more descriptive and searchable. The bottom line is that "Nesting Bird" received nine more bids and sold for $100 more than "Happy Battle."

Master Marketeer's Trick of the Trade: Reserve Price Auctions

A reserve price is the *hidden* minimum price at which a seller will let go of an item. The reserve price is kept secret from the public, enabling a seller to generate more bids. Some sellers set the minimum bid as low as $1. In Figure 3.5, I set the minimum bid at $1 while setting the reserve price at $1 million.

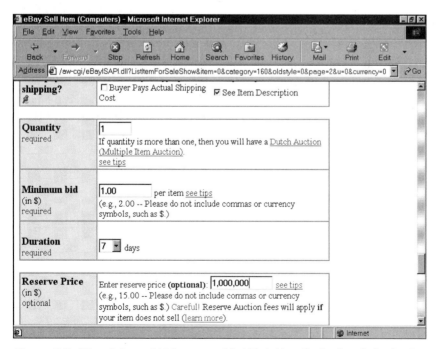

Figure 3.5 *The minimum bid for my petrified Twinkie collection is only $1, but its reserve price is $1 million. I wonder if it will sell?*

If no bid exceeds the reserve price, the auction closes without a winner and the seller retains the merchandise. Reserve price auctions offer an excellent opportunity to establish the intrinsic value of those rare items that come up blank in auction site and shopping bot searches. If an item won't sell at one reserve price, try another—eventually the item find its own value and a new home.

Some sites, like eBay, apply restrictions and tariffs to reserve price auctions, so read the fine print. Master Bidders often avoid reserve price auctions as well. They already know the drill because Master Bidders are Master Marketeers in disguise!

Assignment 6: Study What Sells and Why

You won't believe some of the stuff that gets 30 bids or more on eBay. Check out the Hot Items link under eBay on the *Confessions* CD-ROM. Spend a half-hour or so here discovering what sells. Study the ad of any auction that stands out. When you come across a particularly brilliant ad, examine the auctioneer's other auctions to study his or her technique.

Save the first five hot item pages to the Auction/Research folder on your hard drive and refer to them offline. Don't forget to give them descriptive file names. You can also save auction ads that strike your fancy in that folder to reference later, when you start composing your own ads. Save the HTML as an Entire Web Page to capture the ad's graphics in addition to its text.

CHAPTER 4

Feedback: You're Only as Good as Your Reputation

- ➤ Winning Positive Feedback
- ➤ Negative Feedback and How to Avoid It
- ➤ Assignment 7: Learn the Ground Rules

Feedback at the Internet auction sites is a numerical rating of your reputation and track record that lies within one click of any buyer or seller contemplating an Internet auction transaction with you. As noted in Chapter 3, a buyer's or seller's feedback rating is that number next to his or her name. Clicking the number links you to a page of comments posted by people who have already concluded transactions with that buyer or seller (see Figure 4.1).

This is really mind-boggling when you stop to think about it, and is yet another unique distinction of Internet auctions. Can you name any other form of commerce in which a buyer sets aside the time to write a review of his transaction with a seller? And vice versa—in which a seller takes the time to compose a testimonial for a buyer? It's so honest and polite that it harkens back to the bygone days of Emily Post.

Winning Positive Feedback

There are several steps on the road to earning positive feedback. Take them all and your feedback rating will soar.

- ➤ Be polite
- ➤ Be honest
- ➤ Be prompt
- ➤ Leave positive feedback
- ➤ Ask for positive feedback

Being Polite

To be polite is to delight. In no other walk of life have I encountered a more diverse, pleasant, cross-section of individuals than through Internet auctions.

Figure 4.1 *The feedback page is a must–stop before entering into any transaction on an Internet auction site.*

This week I shipped a humidor to a prince in Saudi Arabia and three Kit-Cat clocks to a housewife in Osaka, Japan. I'm certain neither spoke a word of English, but both transactions went through without a hitch. Would you like to know why? Because English is the universal language of e-mail and the Internet.

If these buyers and I were to bump into each other on a crowded elevator we probably couldn't communicate, yet through the magical medium of Internet auctions we were able to conclude complicated transactions.

E-mail and snail mail are still the preferred means of communication between buyers and sellers in an Internet auction. Feedback is the result of a lot of polite e-mail and envelope licking back and forth. By the end of many transactions I feel like I've gotten to know people; I can almost envision their faces. I want to compliment them, and they often want to compliment me. That's the essence of Internet auction feedback and why it's such a powerful force.

Being Honest

I once made an innocent mistake: I auctioned a Hitachi SR-804 Class G amp-receiver (see Figure 4.2 for a glimpse of this beauty) as a tube amp—but my memory was playing tricks on me. I originally bought it to replace a tube amp, but it was indeed solid state—it had no tubes. Within hours I received a torrent of e-mail, some quite belligerent, demanding that I correct my error; but it was too late. Most sites allow you to amend auctions that have no bids, but my tube amp already had eight. It seems tube amps are quite collectible these days.

I pondered my dilemma. Whatever action I took would first and foremost include a full disclosure and apology. I could close the auction early or allow it to run its course, but in either case I had some explaining to do. So I opened my word processor and composed the following e-mail form letter.

> *Greetings,*
>
> *Thank you for bidding on eBay auction 133557974 for the HITACHI SR-804 AMP. I hope you're more knowledgeable about Hi Fi than I am. During the course of this auction I received e-mail advising me that the SR-804 is a solid-state unit. I researched it on the Internet and found that this appears to be the case. Check the audiophile link*

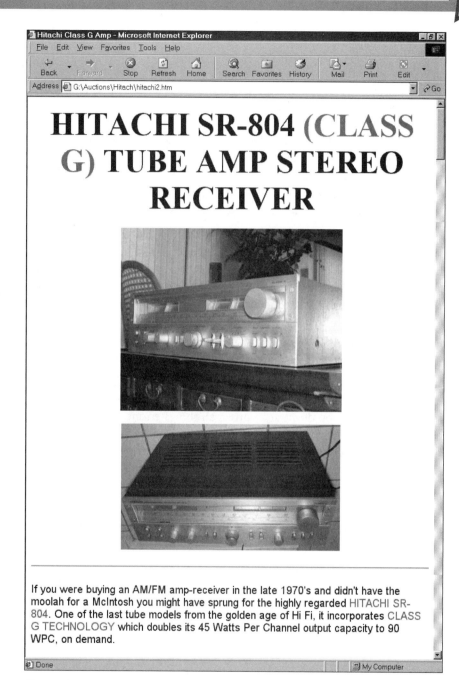

Figure 4.2 *The auction ad for my Hitachi SR-804 Class G amp-receiver*

following my footnote* for complete specs on the Hitachi SR-804 Class G amp-receiver. Please pardon this misrepresentation and any inconvenience it has caused. If you're still interested, kindly let me know.

Michael

*CLASS G

Using two power supplies improves efficiency enough to allow significantly more power for a given size and weight. Class G is becoming common for pro audio designs. [Historical note: Hitachi is credited with pioneering class G designs with their 1977 Dynaharmony HMA 8300 power amplifier and 1978 SR-804 amp-receiver.]

As you can see, I was forthright, polite, and contrite. But I didn't give up on the sale, either. I researched Class G on the Internet and included that footnote, along with the audiophile link on which it appeared. By the end of the auction my old Hitachi had seventeen bids ranging from $40 to $153. Obviously, the majority of these bidders took me at my word that the SR-804 was a tube amp, without doing any research. I bulk e-mailed my *mea culpa* to all the bidders, en masse. Many complimented me on my candor and most were quite understanding. But none were interested in an old solid-state receiver.

Internet auctions provide a certain degree of protection against blunders like mine. The Web is crawling with cyberspace "know-it-alls" whose main mission in life is to swoop down and correct all things erroneous. By the time I e-mailed the high bidder to inform him of my mistake he was already aware that my amp-receiver had no tubes. News travels fast on the Internet! The same person who had corrected me had also e-mailed him.

Hello—I just saw the ad for your Hitachi on EBAY. You have probably already received a wealth of e-mail on the subject, but just in case I thought I should tell you that there are no tubes in that stereo. Those are nice, well built receivers, but are all solid state. If you want to see for yourself, take the four screws out of the cover (2 on each side near the bottom, and maybe one on the back top) and the cover will lift right off starting in the rear. Also, the face is anodized aluminum and not stainless steel. I had a small used stereo buy/sell/repair business back in the '80s into the early '90s and sold several of them. They always seemed to be dependable and looked good.

Good luck on your auction.

Bulk and Form E-Mail

Note how e-mail came to my rescue in this situation. There were 17 bidders but I didn't have to write 17 letters. I only had to write one good one! Nor did I have to e-mail 17 individual bidders. Bulk e-mail allowed me to send the same letter to all of them at once. I'll delve deeper into form and bulk e-mail later. You'll experience firsthand how it is a principal tool of the Internet auctioneer.

In this example of an Internet auction gone awry, the high bidder would have been perfectly within his rights to leave neutral or negative feedback about me. In an Internet auction you can only leave feedback about people with whom you have completed a transaction. In this case, luckily for me, the winner showed some compassion. I'm very proud of my feedback rating—all positives and no negatives—but as this story illustrates, minor transgressions do slip through the cracks.

Being Prompt

E-mail is instantaneous, but the rest of the Internet can be slow as molasses. I'm not just talking about bandwidth, I'm referring specifically to order fulfillment. An Internet auction runs anywhere from three to ten days.

Add another three days to swap e-mail if the auctioneer and the bidder are both prompt, double that if they aren't. Add another week for the seller to receive the buyer's payment, if it's mailed promptly. What form is the payment? If it's a personal check, the seller may wait another week for it to clear. Even if the item ships the next day it could take a week to reach the buyer, the postal service being what it is.

In other words, under optimal conditions the winner of an Internet auction will typically wait 17 to 24 days to receive an item they bid on as much as three to ten days before finding out they won. That, my friends, is *slow*, which is why it's incumbent on both buyer and seller to be prompt, not just with e-mail, but especially when it comes to payment and shipment. Slow e-mail, slow payment, and slow shipping are three of the leading contributors to negative feedback.

Leaving Positive Feedback

The best way to get positive feedback is to leave positive feedback. Lead by example; when a transaction concludes successfully, always take a few extra seconds to register your satisfaction. That's all the time it takes—about as long as it'll take you to look at Figures 4.3 and 4.4.

Asking for Positive Feedback

Last but not least, the second-best way to get positive feedback after you've left it is to ask the party for whom you left it to return the favor. In my experience approximately one person in three leaves positive feedback for new products I sell, and one person in five left it back in my closet-mining days. I make a habit of leaving positive feedback for everyone who pays me.

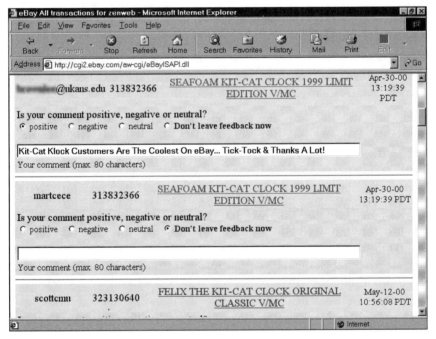

Figure 4.3 *What goes around comes around.*

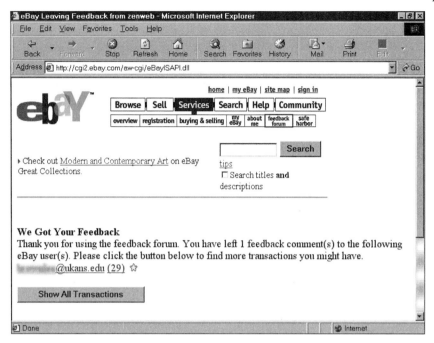

Figure 4.4 *Feedback is the equivalent of Internet auction karma.*

Negative Feedback and How to Avoid It

I must confess that I'm a real wimp when it comes to leaving negative feedback. I've only left it once, and then went into a guilt trip over it, even though this individual really deserved it. I'd just attained the magical feedback rating of 10 on eBay; A positive feedback rating of 10 entitles you to the keys to the kingdom; you're allowed to run *feature* and *Dutch* auctions.

> **Feature auction or category feature auction**. Your auction will appear on the first page in its product category or on the auction site's home page. Prominent placement guarantees that more people will view your auction. This form of advertising costs $15 to $125 extra.

> **Dutch auction**. An auction in which two or more identical products are sold at the same price.

One of my first Dutch auctions was for a product called Profit-Master, a compilation disk of useful hyperlinks to free products, services, and information. Chalk it up to beginner's luck, but the auction got eight bids. One was from a deadbeat we'll call Chuck.

A *deadbeat* is a person who bids on an item and doesn't follow through. Deadbeats don't answer their e-mail and they don't send payment. They simply disappear and leave you hanging while the auction site takes its cut. Chuck was my first deadbeat and I got in a real tizzy over it. I e-mailed him eight times; a month passed and I got zilch back. I bellyached to eBay and they advised me to register a complaint on the Feedback Forum. One morning I woke up in a foul mood and took their advice.

> *User: zenweb (107) Date: 07/23/99, 11:08:41 PDT*
>
> *Complaint: A DEADBEAT! Won my auction and never responded to numerous e-mails.*

Chuck responded immediately to my feedback.

> *Response: I sent payment timely, never got the product, and never received any e-mails.*

Chuck didn't send payment and contrary to his statement, he had received numerous e-mails. He acknowledged this a few days later when he e-mailed me.

> *Sorry for not answering sooner. I get so much junk e-mail every day, about 100. I did not see ebay in your title and thought it was all junk mail. I still want your product. Please give payment instructions. Chuck.*

If Chuck hadn't admitted his guilt, I might have felt worse. To keep things strictly aboveboard I instructed him to bid on Profit-Master again in an ongoing auction. He did so and this time paid promptly. He then requested positive feedback, which I left.

> *User: zenweb (107) Date: 08/10/99, 10:36:50 PDT*
>
> *Praise: Chuck contacted me after e-mail mishap. I retract my former statement about him being a Deadbeat.*

That's not the end of the story. A few months later I received the following e-mail from Bryan, a complete stranger.

Hi—I noticed your feedback regarding Chuck. Did you ever resolve the issue, and if so, how? I sent payment ($79).... It was received and cashed, but I have received absolutely no information in return. Not even an acknowledgment. My numerous e-mails have gone unanswered. Please advise. Thanks!

Bryan

I e-mailed Bryan the gist of what transpired, which led me to investigate Chuck's feedback. It stunk! His rating of 16 was made up of nineteen positive, three neutral, and three negative comments, including mine. Here are the less glowing reviews.

User: XXXX (15) Date: 10/10/99, 13:16:04 PDT Neutral: hard to contact but worked out good would buy from again.

User: XXXX (30) Date: 08/28/99, 18:16:35 PDT

Neutral: No payment for winning the bid. Stay away from this one!!!!!

Response: I sent payment don't know what happened.

User: XXX@excite.com (-1) Date: 08/23/99, 09:50:51 PDT

Complaint: A RIPOFF ARTIST! Chuck will NOT return calls or e-mail. Still don't have program.

Response: He sent incomplete order, I couldn't contact him, Left N.F. before contacting me.

User: zenweb (107) Date: 07/23/99, 11:08:41 PDT

Complaint: A DEADBEAT! Won my auction and never responded to numerous e-mails.

Response: I sent payment timely, never got the product, and never received any e-mails.

User: XXXldon (17) Date: 06/11/99, 18:15:11 PDT

Complaint: Did not reply to 4 e-mails, did not make payment.

Response: He never gave me a chance to buy his product, I was out of town for 3 days.

This feedback is a red flag! Six out of twenty-five transactions were negative or neutral. That's 25 percent. Chuck is bad news and this kind of feedback is indicative of a person you should go out of your way to avoid.

I'm a little older now, and a little wiser, and I have a confession to make. I've had dozens of deadbeats since Chuck, and I didn't bother to leave negative feedback about any. It detracts from my enjoyment, distracts from more positive endeavors, and I don't like getting into tizzies. Deadbeats are a by-product of Internet auctions and an unavoidable reality. Whether or not you choose to leave negative feedback is entirely up to you. At the risk of contradicting myself, I would advise that you do—you could potentially spare someone the bad experience you had.

This is purely an empirical observation so I can't quote exact percentages, but in my experience eBay has the fewest deadbeats. Amazon has slightly more and Yahoo! has the most. I believe this is due in part to eBay imposing the most stringent requirements on sellers—anyone can hold a featured or Dutch auction on Yahoo! or Amazon, whereas eBay makes you earn the privilege. eBay was the first auction site, is presently the largest, and—in my opinion—at the moment has the most reputable user base.

Safe Harbor and Insurance

eBay has a department with the warm and fuzzy title of Safe Harbor where you can lodge complaints by e-mail. In return you receive an empathetic reply informing you that you're pretty much on your own. Here's an excerpt from Safe Harbor's form reply to my complaint about Chuck.

> Hello,
>
> Thank you for writing. We are sorry to hear that one of your buyers has backed out of completing a transaction. We realize that although this situation is rare because of our feedback system, it is disappointing if it happens to you.
>
> Have a great day!
>
> eBay Customer Support
>
> Safe Harbor Investigations Team

eBay's heart is in the right place, however. Every eBay user is covered by insurance. If you pay for an item and never receive it (or if you received the item, but it's less than what you expected), eBay will reimburse buyers up to $200, less a standard $25 deductible. This doesn't address the transactions on eBay that are less than $25 or are big-ticket items, but it's certainly a step in the right direction.

Rules for Avoiding Negative Feedback

In the end, there are three rules to follow in order to stay negative feedback-free. You've heard them before:

➤ Never misrepresent what you're selling.

➤ Always tell the truth.

And the golden rule in Internet auctions, just as in life: *Do unto others as you would have them do unto you.*

Assignment 7: Learn the Ground Rules

If you know the rules of the auction site and you abide by them, chances are good that all of your feedback will be of the positive variety. Click on Rules and Regulations on the *Confessions* CD-ROM under Internet Auction Sites and read the guidelines, limitations, restrictions, and rules of each auction site with which you're registered.

Save them in the Auction/Research folder on your hard drive so you can refer to them later if you have a question.

CHAPTER 5

Navigation and Negotiation: Are Dutch Auctions Held in Holland?

The best way to learn about Internet auctions is firsthand, by bidding and selling. You'll get plenty of experience doing that in the next section of the book, "Experimentation." A slew of Internet auction books have recently hit the market that are little more than cut-and-paste jobs: screen-shots of auction sites along with log-on instructions. This is counterproductive! Going to a site and clicking around for yourself is far more instructive than is reading about it in a book. The most important thing to realize now is that navigating the major auction sites is basically self-explanatory. Despite minor cosmetic differences in their GUIs (*Graphical User Interfaces*), in essence they work the same way (see Table 5.1).

Sizing Up the Sites

My "Wizard of Oz" reference in Table 5.1 is no exaggeration. The employee-to-revenue ratio of an Internet auction operation—the sum of the revenues generated, divided by the number of employees—is mind-boggling! eBay, the only company that discloses this sort of data, has 138 employees. In the first three fiscal quarters of 1999, eBay generated revenues of $150.8 million. The employee-to-revenue ratio is a whopping $1,092,753 per employee. It would be one thing if they sold big-ticket items, but this income was generated by collecting a paltry 2.5 to 5 percent commission on millions of individual sales, a majority of which are under $20. These 138 individuals make up the entire eBay empire—the whole shebang including the technology, Web site, database, almost 4 million auctions a month, Wall Street, the media, PR, advertising, lawyers, secretaries, accountants, bookkeepers, janitors, and the company cafeteria. You get the picture. With manpower spread this thin there aren't many people around to field phone calls!

Table 5.1 Common Components of the Major Auction Sites

Account Management Tools	Every site provides tools that allow you to manage your account, view recent activity, and update personal information.
Auction Management Tools	Every site provides a central location to monitor and manage your current auctions and bids; this is generally linked to your Account Tools.
Help	Help is only a click or two away, so be brave! The major sites all have user-friendly, intuitive help.
Bid	Bidding is a no-brainer! Being a Master Bidder is a lifelong calling.
Sell	Listing an auction can seem intimidating at first. But once you grasp the alphabet soup of technobabble: HTML, FTP, GIF, JPG, and URL, you'll wonder what all the fuss was about. Anyone can sell something, but being a Master Marketeer is an art and a craft!
Search	Sooner or later, every model of every brand of every product under the sun will be auctioned on the Internet. More than likely, it already has been. Quick, think of anything! Now search eBay. It was there, wasn't it?
Browse by Category	eBay presently has 4,300 separate product categories. Every site provides a page where you can browse the auctions by category, but only eBay has the chutzpah to advertise its numbers!
Feedback	Every auction site provides a feedback system that lets users rate the reliability of other members.
Site Management	Services vary, but every site provides e-mail links to management. You'll have to search far and wide to find phone numbers, however. Behind the facade, even the biggest auction sites are understaffed "Wizard of Oz" operations.

eBay is the Cadillac of auction sites, Amazon is like a Honda Accord, and Yahoo! reminds me of an old VW bus (see Table 5.2). They're like three peas in a pod, however. Most professional auctioneers use Amazon and Yahoo! as adjuncts to eBay; they list their auction on all three sites, using eBay as their headquarters. Buyers also consider eBay the major league of auction sites and head there first. This has a real impact on the bottom line—at the end of the month I derive 80 percent of my auction revenues from eBay and 20 percent from the others combined. A few months ago I stopped listing auctions on Amazon altogether because that 4000-character limitation was giving me high blood pressure. When I registered my displeasure with them by e-mail in the form of a mock resignation, Amazon sent me this polite and heartfelt form apology.

> *Thanks for contacting us at Amazon.com.*
>
> *In addition to our large selection, one of the benefits we'd like to offer our customers is convenience, and we have not met that standard in this case. Please accept our sincere apologies. We do appreciate your business, and would like to give you a $10.00 gift certificate for use toward your next Amazon.com order.*

The upshot is that I bought a Macy Gray CD with the Amazon gift certificate and haven't listed an auction on their site since.

Table 5.2 Differences Between the Major Auction Sites

	eBay	Amazon	Yahoo!
Basic Listing	.25	.10	Free
Headline	45 characters	80 characters	80 characters
HTML Character Limitation	None	4000 characters	None
Graphic File Limitation	None	100K file size limit	3 graphics only
Dutch/Feature Listing Restriction	Feedback rating of 10 plus	None	None
Deadbeat Bids*	Less than 10%	Around 25%	35% to 40%
Ease of Use**: Web site (1-5)	4	4	4
Ease of Use: Listing (1-5)	2	1	3
Custom Ads HTML (1-5)	5	1	3

*As stated in the last chapter, the Deadbeat stats are empirical.
**The rating scale is 1-5, with 5 being the easiest to use.

In all fairness to Yahoo!, I must clarify that I don't list Feature auctions on their site like I do on eBay. The high percentage of deadbeats on Yahoo! deters me. I have listed auctions on Lycos as well, but few sales have resulted.

I give eBay high marks for effort. They attract the most reliable bidders and reputable sellers. 25 to 30 thousand people derive a full time income on eBay. I also give eBay kudos for empowering these people to go into business for themselves. On the other hand, when eBay crashes, Wall Street clucks its collective tongue, the stock tumbles, and millions of Internet auctions are lost in cyberspace.

eBay does suffer from a split personality. It strives to be a democratic community, but a minor or even erroneous infraction of the rules reveals a Jekyll and Hyde personality. To compensate for their critical manpower shortage, eBay relies on form scenarios to deal with so-called rules infractions. This can result in banishment to e-mail purgatory! I've experienced it up close and personal, even though I was innocent. That's how I met the Sheriff of eBay, who you'll meet in Chapter 13.

Browser versus Browser

Another beef I have with eBay is frustrating software errors which make it next to impossible to list new auctions with Microsoft Internet Explorer. I struggled with this for months because Internet Explorer was my default Web browser. I would fill in the sell item screen, hit the submit button and repeatedly receive the error message shown in Figure 5.1.

The situation became so intolerable that I dashed off an e-mail complaint to eBay Tech Support. They sent back the following response.

Hello,

Thank you so much for taking the time to write to eBay. I'm very sorry that you're having troubles listing items. This error seems to happen primarily with Internet Explorer browsers, but Netscape seems to work fine from the same computer. Would you please download a copy of Netscape as a backup? I will send a report of this problem to the appropriate department. We certainly want this problem to be fixed too. If you can't sell your items, how would we make money?

eBay Customer Support

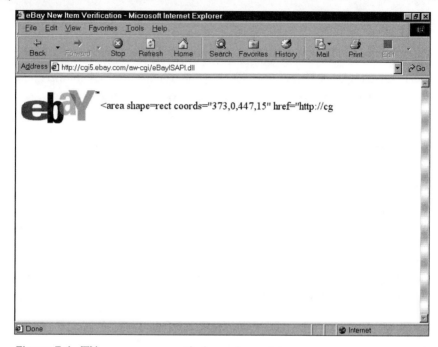

Figure 5.1 *This error screen was the bane of my existence.*

I downloaded Netscape Navigator and haven't had a Server Error since. Problem solved? Not exactly! The problem is that these two programs don't peacefully coexist. When I installed Navigator it became my default Web Browser, *by default*; very sloppy execution on Netscape's part! I should have been given a choice. At any rate, it wreaked havoc with my HTML editor, Microsoft FrontPage 2000, and with Windows. When I changed my default Web browser back to Internet Explorer, I began to get error messages. But alas, the error messages were in error! When I clicked OK, Internet Explorer performed as it should. I turned to Microsoft for help.

> *Incident #: SRZ000122000550*
>
> *Date: Jan 22 2000, 22:27:57 GMT*
>
> *Source: Web Response Status: CLOSED*
>
> *Subject: IE Reset Server Errors on eBay - plus - IE file error messages*
>
> *Files: WR000122142759.zip*
>
> *Contact: m weber*

Hi

I have two related problems.

1) I get Server Reset Errors whenever I list auctions on eBay using IE. They don't happen with Navigator.

2) When I downloaded Navigator it became my default browser, which I didn't want. Please tell me how to correct this file error problem and avoid the IE reset errors with eBay.

Michael

NOTE

You can examine the entire report by clicking Microsoft Incident Report on the *Confessions* CD-ROM.

This is what's known as an Incident Report. Microsoft Tech Support posts replies on the Internet, providing its users with step-by-step guidance on resolving their problems. Microsoft helped me fix my registry problem first; it took numerous steps, including uninstalling and reinstalling Internet Explorer several times. This torture could have been avoided if Netscape had simply given me the choice of which Web browser I preferred as my default browser in the first place. I implore software developers to make the user's "default preference" a mandatory part of any install routine!

After resolving my registry problems I pressed Microsoft to resolve the server errors I encountered listing auctions on eBay and Yahoo! with Internet Explorer. I chanted the magic words: "I'm writing a book." Microsoft then got in touch with eBay and the truth finally came out.

eBay admitted to Microsoft that when it developed its site it was tested with Netscape Navigator but not with Microsoft Internet Explorer. The answer is as silly and simple as that! As of this writing neither company has fixed the problem, although both are aware of it.

What does all this have to do with your Internet auctions? As I discovered the hard way, you may need two Web browsers—Netscape Navigator for compatibility and Internet Explorer for advanced features.

The bottom line is, don't fix it if it ain't broke! If your Web browser works, disregard the following advice: If you experience Server Reset or other error messages while listing your auctions using Microsoft Internet Explorer, list your auctions with Netscape Navigator instead.

The Dutch Auction Paradox

Dutch auctions aren't held in Holland and to be perfectly honest with you, I'm not even sure why they're called Dutch auctions. The only hard and fast truth is that in a Dutch auction more than one identical item is sold at the same price. Dutch auctions are more apt to be run by professional sellers, but this isn't always the case. Dutch merchandise is also more likely to be new, but this, too, is not always true.

Not every seller can run a Dutch auction. Yahoo! and Amazon let anyone hold a Dutch auction, but eBay makes you earn the privilege with two month's membership in good standing and a positive feedback rating of ten.

I love Dutch auctions! Because I have a warehouse full of merchandise standing behind me, Dutch auctions are the only kind I list these days. Each auction is for fifty items, so fifty bidders can potentially win. However, I'm not charged an insertion fee for each listing! eBay imposes a $2 ceiling on multiple listings regardless of the number of items listed. I didn't discover this invisible perk until I started listing Dutch auctions. To this day I haven't been able to find it documented on their site. Amazon and Yahoo! charge nothing to list multiple items.

The Category Conundrum

Before you can list an auction, you must figure out which category to list it in. In the short time it took me to write this book, eBay's Product Categories swelled from 1000 to 4,320. The importance of what category you place an item in cannot be overstated. At the end of the day, your choice of category can ultimately be more important than the quality of your headline or the content of your ad!

I sell Kit-Cat Klocks in several categories, a number of which aren't obvious. In addition to listings in "Collectibles—Clocks" and its assorted subcategories, I've had great success selling them in "Everything Else—Baby Items," "Everything Else—Home Furnishings," and "Collectibles—Cats." On different occasions I've listed this one product in dozens of categories!

The General Category

You'll soon discover that several categories, and almost every subcategory, have a category called "General." I only list Featured auctions in the "General" category, and I recommend that you do the same or avoid this category altogether. The reasons are twofold. The first reason is that, at the most, auction sites like eBay list fifty auctions per page. If you were to list an old African manuscript under "Antiques & Art—General" for example, you'd have to compete with 10,973 other listings. Your auction would be lost in a sea 220 Web pages deep and be submerged near the bottom of the list for over half its duration. The odds that your headline will catch the eye of an interested browser are extremely low throughout most of your auction's duration.

An investment of $16.95 to list your manuscript as a boldface "Featured category auction" in "Antiques & Art—General" will dramatically tip the odds in your favor. "Featured category auctions" guarantee that your listing will always appear on the first page, or at least near it. If a category has over 50 Featured listings, the listings will spill onto a second Featured page and get rotated to the first page several times a day. Now, everyone browsing in this popular category will see your auction right near the top!

Is there a way around having to pay $16.95 to get your African manuscript auction to appear on the first page in an appropriate category? In this example, the answer is yes! Study the following Antiques & Art category and its subcategories:

Antiques & Art (136596)

General (10973)	Maritime (1217)
Antiquities (3781)	Medical (908)
Architectural (5141)	Metalware (5324)
Art:Fine (39681)	Musical Instruments (908)
Asian Antiques (6154)	Primitives (4041)
Books, Manuscripts (5121)	Reproductions (1649)
Ceramics (3629)	Science Instruments (827)
Ethnographic (4177)	Silver (9122)
European (1060)	Silver Plate (3762)
Folk Art (3947)	Textiles, Linens (7852)
Furniture (3960)	Toleware (625)
Glass (3285)	Woodenware (2137)
Maps, Atlases (1631)	Antiques (post-1900) (5770)

If you delve one level deeper into the "Books, Manuscripts" category, this is what you'll find.

Books, Manuscripts (5121)

General (2538)	English (391)
African (37)	European (267)
American (1714)	Latin American (26)
Asian (98)	

There it is, right under your nose! The "African" category for only has 37 listings, so your headline will appear on the first page. And depending on its minimum bid, the listing could cost as little as a quarter!

The second reason to avoid "General" category listings is they're often *too* general, as exhibited by the GI Joe listings in the "Action Figure" category below.

GI Joe (6610)

General (661)	3 3/4" (2304)
12 Inch (2255)	3 3/4" Accessories (407)
12" Accessories (983)	

Assignment 8: Categorization and Navigation

Follow the Category link under eBay on the *Confessions* CD-ROM to behold what four 4000+ categories look like. The number next to each category indicates the number of listings in that category. Save the category overview in the Auction/Research folder on your hard drive and study it often.

While on eBay, click "Site Map" above the banner and save the map in the Auction/Research folder on your hard drive, too. Now click the other links above eBay's banner. Save any page that you think is appropriate for later reference. Don't forget to use descriptive file names!

NOTE

Although eBay has the most comprehensive list of categories, you should repeat this assignment for every auction site with which you're registered to discover what's available on that site.

PART II

Experimentation: Closet Mining

CHAPTER 6

Nothing Could Be Finer Than to Be a Closet Miner

To be an Internet auctioneer you must *see* like one. Look around the room you're in. Notice how cluttered it's become. Wouldn't that table look nicer with a few less chotchkes? Perhaps the room would look better without that table entirely. Are you displaying your treasures in their best light or are objects clashing in space and competing for attention? There are fond memories associated with much of this stuff. But do you really need it, or is it just collecting dust? Over time, we all become a little complacent. We don't look at our possessions—we overlook them. You must view your environment through the eyes of an interior decorator to be a good Internet auctioneer!

One of the great collateral benefits of Internet auctions is that you'll reclaim invaluable living space. The term *closet mining* doesn't pertain strictly to closets; it includes drawers, dressers, shelves, cabinets, commodes, hutches, cupboards, bureaus, chests, trunks, armoires, attics, cellars, garages, and every other nook, cranny, and room in your house. You're about to embark on a treasure hunt. Virtually every object you encounter has an inherent value established by a previous Internet auction. There are collectors, traders, and users out there who value your possessions more than you do waiting for you on the Internet. What are *you* waiting for?

One Man's Trash Is Another Man's Treasure

One of the first things you'll discover about Internet auctions is that there are collectors of virtually everything. I dare say if you could figure out how to package it, a few dust collectors would come out to bid. Do you remember how I paid for that new printer by auctioning the parts of a broken one? In my wildest dreams I'd never have guessed that would be possible. You'll never know what something's worth until you put it on the auction block.

I had a broken camcorder, the RCA PRO 880 HI-8 shown in Figure 6.1, that *Consumer Reports* once named "Camcorder Of The Year." I loaned it to an actress friend to rehearse a play she was in and it came back DOA. She was a good sport and paid to have it fixed. But shortly after I got it back, the viewfinder went on the fritz.

I don't put much stock in astrology but there is one tenet to which I adhere, called "Mercury in retrograde." It's a phase of the moon in which all things mechanical are susceptible to breakdown. As far as I was concerned, this camcorder's Mercury was in permanent retrograde! I decided to put it on the auction block. I figured I'd be lucky to get fifty bucks for the thing, even though it originally cost me over $1500.

As you can see, I'm a proponent of truth in advertising. Right on top in big bold red letters, the headline reads BROKEN CAMCORDER -- NEEDS SERVICE -- SOLD AS-IS! To my utter amazement, my "worthless" camcorder got 13 bids, topping out at $202. Unfortunately, the high bidder backed out, but I still wound up getting $163.88 for the broken camcorder from the second highest bidder. As with the broken printer, I would never have imagined a broken *anything* could fetch so much. Who would buy a broken camcorder? Here is the e-mail from the winning bidder.

> *Michael,*
>
> *I received the camcorder yesterday. It arrived in excellent shape. I hoped that the problem was just in the viewfinder. However, the actual camera video is bad. I was able to trace the problem to bad capacitors in the camera. These types of capacitors are known to develop problems over time. The good news is that they are inexpensive. The bad news is that they require A LOT of labor time to replace. I "held" a couple of physically larger capacitors in place and the video cleared up nicely. So currently the camera is completely apart and I'm waiting for an order of n capacitors. I'll probably just replace all of them that I can easily get to. I estimate about 20—30; but they only cost about 0.30 each. However, it will take SEVERAL hours to change them and get the unit back together again. I registered a positive on eBay for you. Nice dealing with you.*
>
> *Andy*

Figure 6.1 *My broken camcorder broke my heart.*

You get to meet people you'd never know from places you'd never go! That's the uniqueness of Internet auction. I cashed out, reclaimed valuable living space, and got a bonus—a dissertation on broken camcorders. Andy got what he wanted, too: a camcorder to fix. Multiply the quality of this experience by dozens of transactions, one for each auction, and you'll have a glimpse of what awaits you as a closet miner.

The Internet Auction Riptide

Internet auctions are synergistic: one thing leads to another. You dive in and get swept away. The success of the camcorder auction went to my head—I had a couple of other cameras I didn't use either, and like all aspiring Internet auctioneers, I wanted to add a digital camera to my collection. Voilà, a riptide is born! At the bottom of my closet, buried beneath a bunch of old sneakers, was my first 35mm SLR, a Pentax Spotmatic. I hadn't taken a picture with it since replacing it with a Nikon F 15 years earlier. Out of sight, out of mind! I hadn't removed it from its case or given it a fleeting glance ever since. It might have remained there, hermetically sealed in perpetuity, if not for the success of my camcorder auction.

I dusted off the case and took the old Spotmatic out. As I clutched it in my hands, my head swam with memories. I was a teenager once again, in Prospect Park snapping pictures of my grandfather; I had learned the basics of photography on this camera. And there was a bonus buried in the bottom of the case: two lenses I'd completely forgotten about. I bought a new battery, popped in a roll of film, and discovered that—unlike a couple of my earlier auction offerings—the Spotmatic actually worked!

Next came due diligence. I researched "Spotmatic" on the Internet and discovered to my delight that Spotmatics are highly collectible. If I played my cards right I might even get what I originally paid for it, if only I could remember what that was! Are you aware that there are dozens of Web sites and stores devoted to nothing but Pentax Spotmatics? I wasn't. There are also repair shops that specialize in supplying Spotmatic parts and fixing them. It turns out that I didn't have your ordinary garden variety Spotmatic, either. I had a rare, black, top–of–the–line "Professional" model. I took some glamorous photos of it and worked them them into the ad in Figure 6.2.

RARE BLACK PENTAX SPOTMATIC - Microsoft Internet Explorer

File Edit View Favorites Tools Help

Back Forward Stop Refresh Home Search Favorites History Mail Print Edit

Address G:\Auctions\Spotmatic\Spotmatic1.htm

HONEYWELL PENTAX
SPOTMATIC

RARE BLACK BODY - ASAHI SUPER TAKUMAR 1:2/55 LENS

EXCELLENT WORKING CONDITION!

THE SPOTMATIC DESERVES IT'S PLACE IN HISTORY... NOT AS A COLLECTIBLE TO BE PUT ON THE SHELF AND ADMIRED, BUT AS A TRUE WORKHORSE TO BE TAKEN DOWN AND USED!

Rare Black Body Professional Model Honeywell Pentax Spotmatic 35mm SLR with original Asahi 55mm Super Takumar f1:2/55 lens. Some brassing and minor wear to the body but the camera and lens are in excellent working condition. Film speeds 20 to 1600, shutter speeds 1 sec. to 1/1000 and B.

This is one of the best cameras in the world to learn and master photography with. Its operation is extremely simple; battery powered needle metering and manual setting of the aperature and shutter speed. The construction of this camera out-classes many of today's current "high-end" cameras and is as rugged as a Nikon F4. For general shooting the Spotmatic performs just as well as its modern counterparts.

The Spotmatic takes the famous screw mount lenses, which are perhaps the most underrated and overlooked lenses on the market. The optics are truly suberb - the equal of today's modern lenses, but at a fraction of the price.

The Spotmatic's mechanical shutter, with proper care, will last forever. Due to the popularity of this camera, many repair shops still stock parts and service it.

Payment by Money or Order Cashier's Check... Personal Checks Must Clear

Done   My Computer

Figure 6.2 *I parted with the camera, but not the fond memories that it provided.*

I'm proud of this ad; it projects a sense of history. Notice how I used research to sell the camera. By the time you finish reading it you should regard the Spotmatic as a legendary camera, which it is. After combining the proceeds I received from this auction and that of the broken camcorder, I had enough money to buy a new digital camera!

These Internet auction stories are just the salt on the peanut. To be a successful Internet auctioneer you must first think and see like one. You must mine your own closets, unearth your own treasures, and get swept up in your own riptides.

What Sells?

Everything sells if it's priced right! Here are the results of a few of my more eventful auctions.

Item	Minimum Bid	Reserve Price	Bids	High Bid
Atari Portfolio Palmtop Computer	$9.99	$99.99	15	$107.50
Atari Portfolio Parallel Port	$9.99	$29.99	5	$40.00
Bob Dylan CD-ROM Highway 61	$9.99	$19.99	11	$48.50
Tiffany Buffalo Bill Belt Buckle	$35.00	0	8	$82.00
IBM Printer Used 4MB RAM Chip	$9.99	0	6	$48.00
IBM Printer Used Toner Cartridge	$19.99	0	17	$71.00
Banned est Seminar Book	$9.99	$24.99	3	$38.00
Fuji TW-300 35mm Compact Camera	$19.99	$49.99	4	$52.50

Item	Minimum Bid	Reserve Price	Bids	High Bid
Dunhill Roll-a-gas Butane Lighter	$25.00	$89.99	7	$102.51
Microsoft Encarta DVD-ROM	$9.99	$18.99	7	$36.02
Windows 95 Upgrade CD-ROM	$9.99	$19.99	11	$46.50

Two of these auctions had unforeseen ramifications, and provide a useful insight into the kind of auctions you should avoid.

Banned—Rare est Seminar Book

I broke one of eBay's cardinal rules by using the word *banned* in this auction's headline. It was an innocent mistake on my part, but eBay was within its rights to pull the plug on this auction, and it did. The book in question, *est: Playing the Game the New Way*, is one of my favorites. According to the book jacket its author, Carl Frederick, was no longer affiliated with est (Erhard Seminar Training). The book jacket goes on to read: "This book is the author's transformation of the incredible Erhard Seminars Training experience into words."

Werner Erhard wasn't pleased to hear that a former trainer had usurped and published the very ideas he charged $500 a head to hear at his seminars. Shortly after its publication in 1974, Erhard sued, the book vanished, and few copies remained in circulation. I lent mine to so many friends over the years that the pages came loose from the binding. One day my brother saw me reading this tattered old book and decided to locate a first edition for my birthday. That gift led to the auction of my original copy. The day before the auction closed, eBay sent me the following e-mail:

> *Dear Michael,*
>
> *Your auction: XXX714512 BANNED - RARE EST SEMINAR BOOK - GREAT READ! has been ended for the following reason.*
>
> *Listing Policy Violation: INAPPROPRIATE AUCTION TITLE*
>
> *Although you may not be aware of this policy, eBay does not allow the listing of items that have inadequate or inappropriate titles.*

Auction titles that use the following words in an attempt to market or advertise their item: "Prohibited", "Banned", "Illegal", "Outlawed", or any other descriptive word which may bring into question the legality of an item by either governmental or eBay standards. We have ended the auction(s) early and credited your account for the insertion fees.

Regards,

ended@ebay.com

Had I not used the word *banned* in the headline, this auction would have closed without incident. In this particular case, the high bidder contacted me by e-mail after eBay pulled the plug and we concluded the transaction privately. Follow the Listing Policies link under eBay on the *Confessions* CD-ROM for further information on prohibited words and phrases.

Windows 95: A Cautionary Tale

Have you ever read a software agreement? I'd hazard a guess you haven't. You rip open the envelope, whip out the installation disk, and pop it in your CD-ROM drive like everyone else. End of story—until the advent of Internet auctions!

To the software industry's dismay, Internet auctions have established a burgeoning software aftermarket that never existed before. For years I was a slave to the upgrade—Windows 3.1, Windows 95, Windows 98, Windows 2000—I paid over a hundred bucks for each new version. At one point I had three shopping bags filled with old software sitting on my closet floor. Then Internet auctions came along.

For the first time ever I had a viable outlet for obsolete software. Chucking it no longer made economic sense; doing so was the equivalent of throwing away forty or fifty bucks. I paid for these disks—why shouldn't I be able to sell them?

The software industry would argue that selling their software is prohibited by the fine-print boilerplate on the envelope that they acknowledge hardly anybody reads. This hasn't prevented hundreds of thousands of people from auctioning used software on the Internet, however. You can't put the toothpaste back in the tube, and Auction sites have become the de facto Internet destination for software, by buyers and sellers alike.

Software comes in two varieties: legitimate and illegal. Illegal software is unfortunately all too prevalent on most auction sites. By illegal, I mean software that is bootlegged, pirated, copied, or stolen. This software is dangerous, and using it is not only immoral, it's stupid. I can think of no better way to get a computer virus than to install a bootleg software program on your computer.

Of course the scam artists who peddle this garbage don't advertise it as pirated. By the time the victims find out they've been robbed, the check's already been cashed. Now that a CD burner can be had for less than $200, pirating software is easier than ever. Auction sites do make a concerted effort to police software piracy, but the problem has been around a lot longer than they have. Illegal software must be stamped out. If you are a victim, report it to the auction site and software developer immediately, and post negative feedback about the seller.

According to eBay, 99 percent of the software auctioned on the site is legitimate. Legitimate software is manufactured by a developer and purchased by an end user. Here's where the story gets murky. For years, software developers have had it both ways. They sold retail versions of their programs for top dollar out the front door, while dumping OEM, academic discount, and overruns of the same program out the back door for a fraction of the cost.

This practice backfired with a vengeance with the advent of Internet auctions. In 1999, hundreds of thousands of copies of Microsoft Office Pro, the popular $350 office suite, were auctioned for under $25. Some of it was new, some used, and it came in three basic flavors: Retail, OEM, and Academic. It was there because Microsoft flooded the market with it! Office 2000 was just around the corner and Microsoft didn't want to get stuck with a ton of obsolete software. When they realized their flagship product was selling for pennies on the dollar, Microsoft came down on the auction sites. eBay capitulated (a little too easily in my opinion), and I became a target of Microsoft's wrath.

I was auctioning an old Windows Upgrade CD-ROM and Microsoft informed eBay that it was counterfeit. Microsoft was dead wrong. I bought it at Computer City; the disk was genuine Microsoft through and through! How would you like to be greeted by the following e-mail in your in box one morning?

Dear Michael,

eBay has been notified by Microsoft Corporation that the following item you have listed for auction on eBay is believed to be counterfeit or other unauthorized Microsoft product. The item in question is: XXXX20192 MICROSOFT WINDOWS 95 UPGRADE CD-ROM. We take no position on the authenticity of your goods. However, we are required to take any and all action requested by a Content Owner with regard to their works, upon notice. Accordingly, the auction listed above has been terminated. Be advised: The auction of illegal items, including all counterfeit goods, is expressly prohibited and may subject you to criminal prosecution under Federal and State law. Below is information provided by Microsoft.

Respectfully,

ended@ebay.com

In an accusatory and threatening addendum Microsoft added, in part:

Microsoft monitors the Internet to identify sites where pirated software products are being made available, and take action to stop their unlawful distribution. This process led us to your auction on eBay. Microsoft believes that the product offered in this auction is not a genuine Microsoft product.

Being cognizant of the piracy problem, I wrote this blunder off to an innocent mistake on Microsoft's part. Unfortunately, Microsoft left no wiggle room for the presumption of innocence. Their tone was overzealous and tactics heavy-handed. Nor has this approach prevented a torrent of Windows 95 CD-ROMs from flooding the Internet auction marketplace. This morning, six months after eBay pulled the plug on that auction, I searched the site for "Windows 95 CD-ROM" and found 297 copies just like it. Some things never change!

Do as I Say, Not as I Did

Should you auction legal software? The answer is no! A software license is called a license because it is a *license*. Many changes have been instituted since I started closet mining back in the Internet auction Dark Ages of 1999. This is one of them. I learn from my mistakes, and this book is structured in part for you to learn from them as well. That's why it's called *Confessions of an Internet Auction Junkie*, not *Runaway Successes of an Internet Auction Junkie!*

I don't want to leave you with the impression that I'm a desperado, or that eBay and Microsoft are Big Brother. To avoid having the plug pulled on your auctions, read again the "Rules & Regulations" stored in the Auction/Research folder on your hard drive. For further information on prohibited, questionable, and infringing items, follow the Prohibited Items link under eBay on the *Confessions* CD-ROM.

Assignment 9: Taking Stock

Put down this book and let the treasure hunt begin! The task before you is simple. With pencil and paper in hand, inventory your personal possessions. Search your closets, drawers, dressers, shelves, cabinets, commodes, hutches, cupboards, bureaus, chests, trunks, armoires, attics, cellars, garages, and every other nook, cranny, and room in your house. When you look at your belongings, think dollar signs! Create a list. Take your time. Catalog everything that has true meaning or significant value—everything you want to keep—by crossing it off the list. There are things you wouldn't part with for the world; I'm not referring to them. I'm referring to the rest. Auction them to the highest bidder!

Assignment 10: Do Due Diligence

A realistic opening bid increases your auction's odds. Before putting anything on the auction block, find its inherent value. Search eBay for the first ten items on your inventory list by brand name, model number, or keyword. Don't forget to search the Closed Auctions section as well. Use eBay because it has the largest searchable database, but search other auction sites as well. Save your search results in your Auction/Research folder. Don't forget to create descriptive filenames!

CHAPTER 7

A Crash Course in Technobabble: Why ASCII?

This is the biggest, baddest, ugliest chapter in the book, but by the time you finish it you'll know everything you need to know about creating effective Internet auction ads. You're going be pleasantly surprised by what some of your closet mining treasures fetch, but they're not going to auction themselves! You need a decent HTML editor and a crash course in technobabble. I'll be as mercifully brief as possible.

The best laid plans of mice and men are subject to Murphy's Law! I chose AOLpress as the HTML editor in this chapter because it was and still is functional and free. AOL stopped supporting AOLpress on June 30, 2000, however. Now, instead of clicking once to install AOLpress directly from the *Confessions* CD-ROM, I'm afraid you'll have to click twice. I sincerely apologize!

To install AOLpress click the AOLpress link on your *Confessions* CD-ROM under Software, download it, and follow the set-up instructions. You'll find many other fine shareware HTML editors there, too. Of course, you're always free to use a personal favorite! As you'll soon see, all HTML editors are basically alike.

NOTE

AOLpress has an excellent tutorial on the Help menu. You can also refer to the Help menu for detailed instructions on the HTML editor's various functions. The auction sites also have instructive HTML tutorials and shareware links. While online, click Tutorials on the *Confessions* CD-ROM. There you will find everything you need to know to create effective Internet auction ads, as well as a foundation for more complicated HTML tasks.

HTML Basics

Before there were editors to automate HTML programming, people had to type long, arcane text commands similar to DOS in order to create Web pages. Now, click a pretty icon and voilà, a fuchsia background! Click another and a picture of whatever you're auctioning appears. Behind the scenes those long and arcane text commands still dictate what you see, but they're hidden from view, so that all you need to do is be creative!

Place the *Confessions* CD in the CD-ROM drive of your computer and locate this very page under Chapter 7. These steps will familiarize you with the operation of an HTML editor. Are we on the same page? Alright!

All HTML editors are basically the same—a cross between a word processor and graphics program. They control how pictures and text are universally displayed on a computer screen over the Internet.

Open AOLpress and you'll see a screen like the one pictured in Figure 7.1. The menu bar and icons across the top control the HTML editor's critical functions. Each has a corollary on the menu bar submenus.

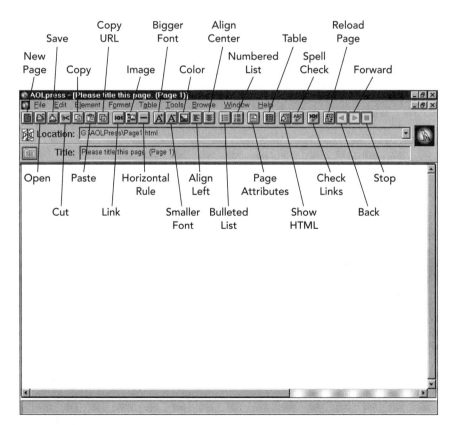

Figure 7.1 *AOLpress' toolbar and icons*

NOTE

You can customize the AOLpress toolbar by accessing Configure Toolbar under Preferences on the Tools menu. The Toolbar will be periodically updated throughout this exercise to display the variety of HTML functions available to you in a standard HTML editor. Hover your mouse pointer over any icon on the toolbar to instantly identify that icon's function.

Using the File and Edit Icons

New Page, Open, Save, Print, Cut, Copy, Paste: if you've ever used a word processor, these functions are familiar. You type some text and then control it by selecting it with your mouse. You can then control the text's size, color, properties, and alignment from the Format menu. Try it!

First, open a new page by selecting File, New and then selecting New Page.

1. Type some text on the page.
2. Select the text with your mouse and you'll get a screen similar to that in Figure 7.2.
3. Click the Format menu (as shown in Figure 7.3) and play with the size, color, and appearance of the text on the Type Style, Type Size, and Type Color submenus.
4. Change the alignment of the text to the right and center of the page by selecting Format, Paragraph (as shown in Figure 7.4).

Using the Image Icon

Your next task is to add a picture. Click the Image icon and select Browse. In the AOLpress\Help\ directory open Startup.Gif; you'll see a screen like the one shown in Figure 7.5. (If you prefer, you can open any GIF or JPG file on your hard drive for this exercise.)

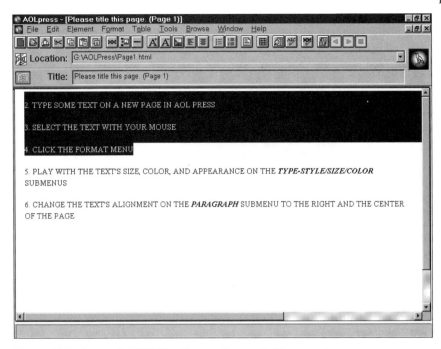

Figure 7.2 *So far the HTML editor works exactly like a word processor.*

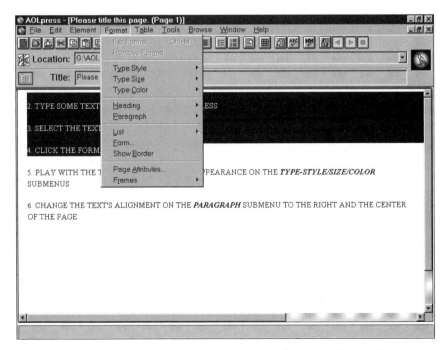

Figure 7.3 *The Format menu has several submenus that control formatting.*

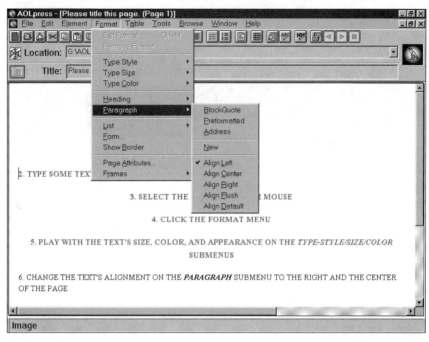

Figure 7.4 *Control text alignment using the options on the Paragraph submenu.*

Figure 7.5 *The page looks like this after adding startup.gif.*

Using the Alignment Icon

Now align the picture using the Align icon. You can use the same procedure to align text.

1. Select Startup.Gif by double-clicking it.

2. Align the image to the center of the page by clicking the Align Center icon.

Using the Page Attributes Icon

You can control page attributes like the background color the same way.

1. Click the "Page Attributes" icon and select a color under Background, Pick, Color (Figure 7.6).

2. Press the Enter (or Return) key four times and the Up arrow twice to get to the next step.

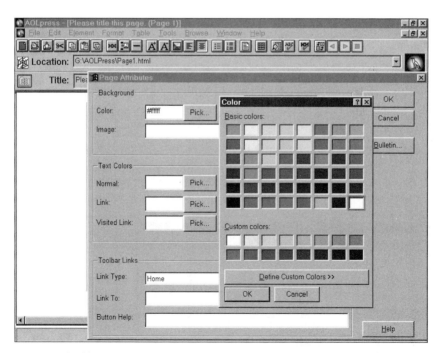

Figure 7.6 *Picking a background color*

Using the Table Icon

Clicking on the Table icon opens a dialog box (Figure 7.7) that allows you to create columns, rows, and picture frames, and is a useful tool for aligning text, images, and doing other neat HTML tricks. A table's border, cell width, color, background, and size are all customizable.

Creating Borders

To place a border around the image you just loaded, follow these steps.

1. Click the Create Table icon and create a table with 1 row and 1 column, and with a size 5 border. Click OK.

2. Select the image by double-clicking it with your mouse then cut and paste it into the table to create a picture in a frame, as shown in Figure 7.8. If you select the image first, and then create the table, the border will automatically surround the image.

Using Grids

You can also use the Table dialog box to set up grids, and even hide the grid lines if you like.

1. Click outside the table and skip down the page a couple of returns.

2. Click the Create Table icon again and create a 2-row, 2-column table with a size 1 border.

3. Type the numbers **1** and **2** in the two cells of column 1 and type a text string of **X's** in each cell of column 2, producing a screen like that in Figure 7.9.

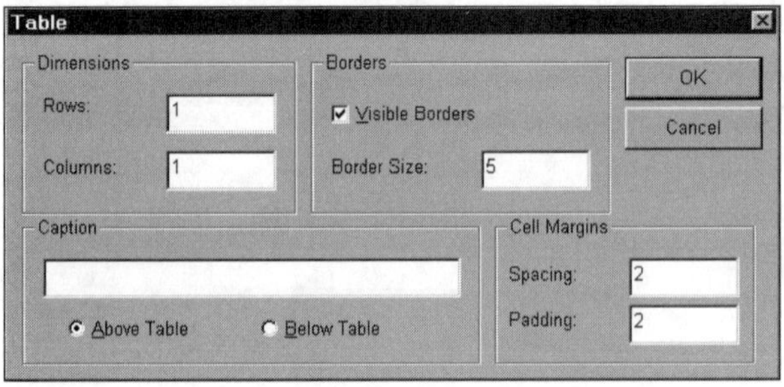

Figure 7.7 *The Table dialog box*

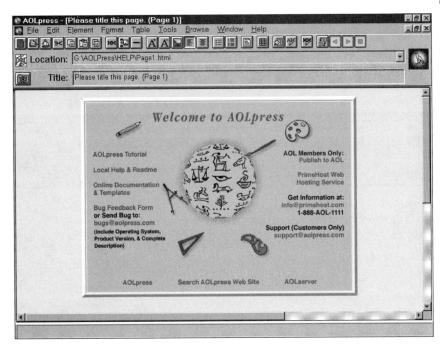

Figure 7.8 *A framed image often appears more polished.*

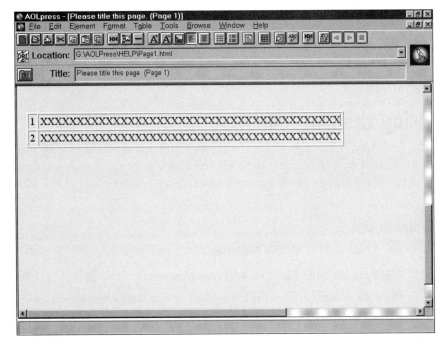

Figure 7.9 *A table with visible borders*

4. Now right-click on the table and change the border size to 0. See how the table keeps the numbers and X's aligned while the grid disappears (Figure 7.10)?

5. Click outside the table and skip down the page.

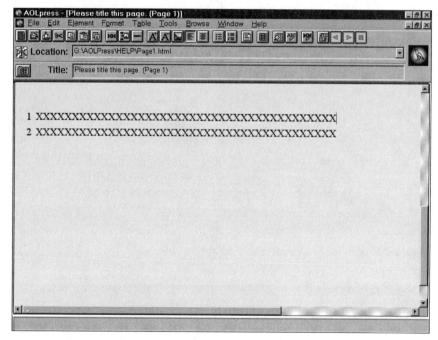

Figure 7.10 *The same table minus borders.*

Using the List Icons

The Table icon is best reserved for lists with multiple columns. To set off text in a different way, click either the Bulleted List icon or the Numbered List icon in AOLpress and you'll get results like those in Figures 7.11 and 7.12.

Bulleted List

To create a bulleted list, do the following:

1. Click the Bulleted List icon and type some text.

2. Press the Enter (or Return) key and another bulleted row appears, as in Figure 7.11.

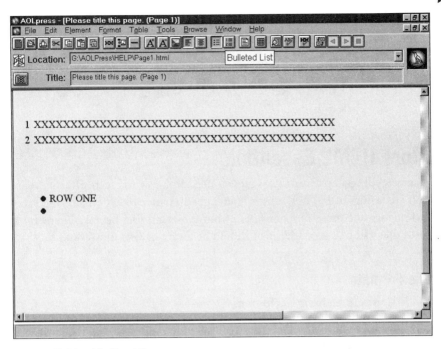

Figure 7.11 *A bulleted list*

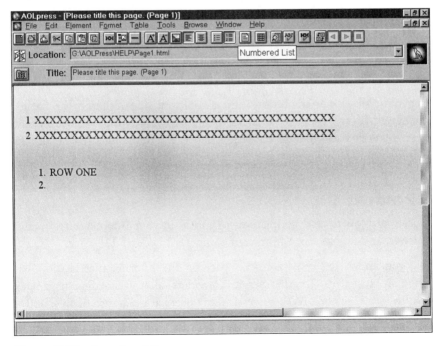

Figure 7.12 *A numbered list*

Numbered List

Create a numbered list in the same way as you would a bulleted list.

1. Click the Numbered List icon and type some text.
2. Press the Enter (or Return) key and another numbered row appears (refer back to Figure 7.12).

More HTML Essentials

The preceding steps encompass all you need to know to create effective auction ads using an HTML editor. You'll get a chance to experience the various nuances of these functions once your closet mining begins. There are a few other HTML essentials you should be aware of first, however.

File Formats

HTML uses three basic file formats:

> ➤ **HTM or HTML.** Web pages are text files stored in HTML format; they have .htm suffixes on PC systems and .html suffixes on Unix-type systems.

> ➤ **GIF.** A file format that works best for line art and graphics with limited colors.

> ➤ **JPG.** A file format that compresses photo-quality images and graphics to a manageable file size. JPG is the format to use for pictures of items to use in your auctions.

Regarding file size on the Internet, there's only one rule of thumb: the smaller the better! JPGs should be no larger than 30K. GIFs, which make excellent page and table backgrounds, can be as small as 2K. Remember that small files that load quickly will result in more people viewing your auctions.

FTP and URL

Question: How do you get pictures to appear in your Internet auction ads? Answer: You upload them from your computer to your FTP space.

Did you know that you have disk space on the Internet that has its own address? Most ISPs (Internet Service Providers) allot users a few megabytes of disk space on their Web servers. Many users are unaware of this, and a majority of those who are aware don't take advantage of it. Internet auction-eers use their FTP space to the hilt!

> **FTP.** The disk space your ISP provides is called an FTP space. It enables users to list files on, retrieve files from, and add files to another computer on the Internet. FTP, short for File Transfer Protocol, is the customary way (protocol) to upload (transfer) files from your computer to the Internet. It's the means by which you can store pictures of whatever you're selling so that those pictures can appear in your auctions.

> **URL.** A URL, short for Uniform Resource Locator, is an Internet address. It's string of characters that identifies the type of file, its name, the computer it's on, and the directories and subdirectories it is in on the Internet. The URL of the White House is http://www2. whitehouse.gov/WH/Welcome.html, for example. The URL of my Kit-Cat page on AOL is http://members.aol.com/urlegant/ default.htm. The URL of the FTP space in which the Kit-Cat files reside is ftp://members.aol.com/urlegant/.

Ask your Internet Service Provider for the URL address of your FTP space. Then you'll be able to place any image of your choosing in your Internet auc-tion ads.

Uploading 101

This is the part of Internet auctions that some people find a bit intimidating. How does a JPG file you upload to one URL (your FTP space) appear on a second URL (the auction site)? The answer and solution are deceptively sim-ple. You link them by specifying the location—the URL address of the JPG file—in your HTML code. Figure 7.13 shows the AOLpress Image dialog box that enables you to do this.

1. Double-click on startup.gif, or select Image on the Element menu. Now right click. The Image dialog box appears with help/startup.gif in the Location text box. Let's change it.

2. Change the Location to my URL address on AOL, HTTP:// MEMBERS.AOL.COM/URLEGANT/STARTUP.GIF, and click OK. You'll get a message about Width/Height. Select Retain.

3. Let's view the underlying HTML code now. Click the Show HTML icon, or click Show HTML on the Tools menu. A HTML screen revealing the HTML code will appear over the Web page.

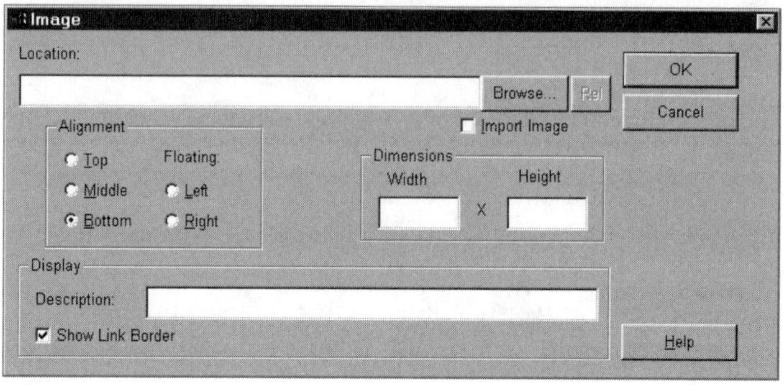

Figure 7.13 *Point a file to an Internet URL address using the Image dialog box*

The underlying HTML code changed from:

```
<IMG SRC="HELP/STARTUP.GIF" WIDTH="505" HEIGHT="350">
```

To:

```
<IMG SRC="HTTP://MEMBERS.AOL.COM/URLEGANT/STARTUP.GIF" WIDTH="505"
HEIGHT="350">
```

Click the Close box on the menu bar in the upper right corner to see the Web page again.

4. Next, I'll upload startup.gif to my FTP space, an easy task using the FTP utility that AOL provides (shown in Figure 7.14.). You'll find several FTP Transfer programs that you can try for free on the *Confessions* CD-ROM, under Software.

5. The final step is to cut and paste the HTML code with the URL location of the JPG or GIF file into the HTML field on the auction site, as shown in Figure 7.15.

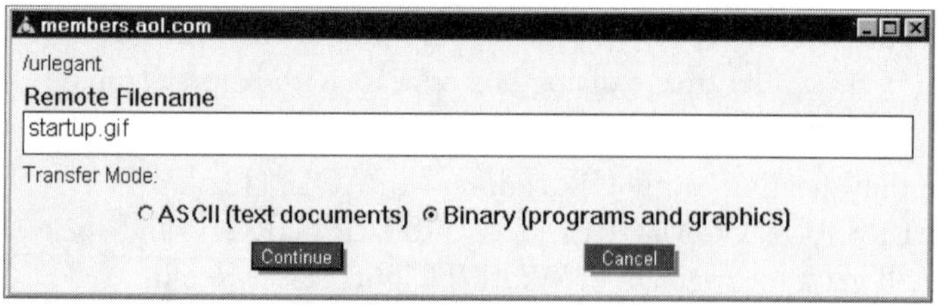

Figure 7.14 *Uploading a file in a few mouse-clicks.*

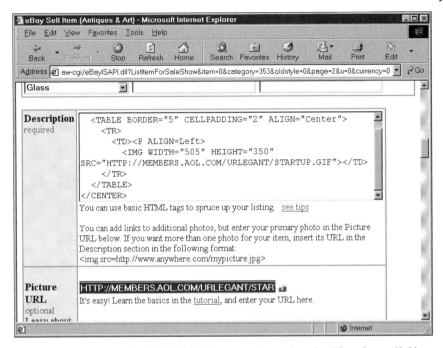

Figure 7.15 *Pasting the URL of the image on the auction site. Note the available eBay tutorial!*

That's all there is to it, so don't be intimidated. Once you get the hang of it you'll be able to upload files and list auctions in five minutes flat!

HTML Secrets

Remember that the T in HTML stands for text. HTML files are nothing but glorified text files with an .htm extension that are associated with the default Web browser on your computer. Your Web browser, HTML editor, and text editor are inexorably connected. Here's a good example of how.

1. Double-click on Readme.htm in the AOLpress directory of your computer (or any other HTM file) within your file manager. The file will open in your Web browser by default.

2. Right-click anywhere on the Web page and click View Source, or
click the View menu and select Source. The source code will open in
Notepad or your default ASCII text editor, because it *is* text. It'll look
something like this:

```
<HTML>
</HEAD>
<BODY BGCOLOR="#ffffff" LINK="#0000b4" VLINK="#18698c">
<P ALIGN=Center>
<A HREF="20.nvm"><IMG BORDER="0" ALT="AOLpress" WIDTH="471"
HEIGHT="101" ISMAP SRC="2.0map.gif" USEMAP="#20map"></A><MAP
NAME="20map">
```

This is the gibberish that all of those neat menus and icons in the HTML
editor are hiding. HTML editors allow you to view and edit source code by
clicking the Tools menu and choosing Show HTML, as you've already
learned. Using this technique, the source code of any Web page on the Internet is open to inspection. If you see a page you like, you can examine its code
by right-clicking View Source on your Web browser's menu. You can also
save a Web page to your hard disk for later examination by clicking Save on
the File menu of your Web browser.

Using the Clipboard

The deeper you get into HTML the more you will rely on your computer's
Clipboard to shuffle images and data between programs and documents. You
can select a passage of text from a Web page, for example, copy it to your
computer's Clipboard, and then paste it into another program. To rid the text
of its formatting before pasting into another program, however, you need to
use a text editor, such as Notepad, SimpleText, or eMacs. Pasting other formats into an HTML editor can wreak havoc.

Using Notepad

Notepad used to be the lowliest program on the Windows totem pole, but the
Internet has plucked it from obscurity. Now it's a Webmaster's best friend.
Anyone who programs HTML relies on a text editor to reduce text to its
purest form, ASCII. It isn't always desirable to import HTML formatting
into your word processor, or word processor formatting into your Web page.
Cutting, pasting, and copying the text in an ASCII text editor—washing it,
so to speak—removes all formatting. A text editor is also a good tool for formatting text. We'll delve deeper into this later in this chapter.

NOTE

The Internet became the phenomenon it is for a single reason: it was designed from the outset to be a cross-platform medium. A Windows PC can talk to a Mac can talk to a Unix machine can talk to a Sun workstation. All computer platforms have one thing in common: ASCII text. ASCII is pure text, devoid of formatting. Hence ASCII, on which HTML is based, became the universal programming language of the Internet because it is the nexus between incompatible computer platforms.

Using Save Picture

Suppose you have a videocassette of the movie *The Godfather* that you'd like to auction. You want Don Corleone's picture to appear in your ad because you know that auctions with pictures garner more bids. You could digitize the cover of the videocassette yourself with a camera, a scanner, or by some other means. Or you can surf over to Amazon.com, type **Godfather** in the search box, and get linked to The Godfather page, shown in Figure 7.16.

1. Right-click over the image of the Godfather in your Web browser. A menu appears.
2. Select the Save Picture As option. The Save Picture dialog box will open (Figure 7.17).
3. Save the GODFATHER.GIF to your hard drive.

NOTE

It's a right-handed world! Clicking the right button on your mouse is the key to unleashing the power of your computer. Unless you're left-handed, like me. I use the term *right-click* generically. If you're a lefty and have rejiggered your mouse, *left-click* to access your mouse menu. Mac users, Control+click is the equivalent of right-clicking.

Explore the various mouse menus of your software and you'll notice that they vary from program to program. Make your mouse an extension of your mind! The deeper you delve into HTML, the more you'll come to depend on it to jockey information between programs and data fields.

Figure 7.16 *Amazon sells* The Godfather, *too.*

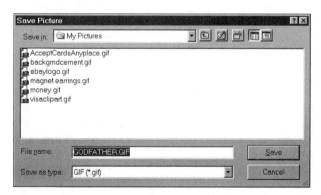

Figure 7.17 *Godfather.gif: From the Internet to your hard drive in a couple of mouse clicks.*

Later you can incorporate the image in the ad for your videocassette auction. Any GIF or JPG image you can view on the Internet can be saved in this manner: photos, backgrounds, borders, even animated GIFs.

Isn't It Plagiarism?

This is one of the great modern philosophical debates. The Internet is not only in the public domain—it's a cross-platform medium based on open source code. The legality of what's copyrightable is a gray area. Amazon.com would have no objection to you downloading and using GODFATHER.GIF, for example. If you downloaded Amazon.com's home page and used it as the home page of another Web site, however, Amazon would object strenuously.

The Internet is an open book. You can download entire pages to your hard disk willy-nilly, and theoretically use them in any way you like. It's all a matter of degree. If you exhibit sound judgment, common sense, and above all, honesty, you can borrow elements from other Web pages and use them without guilt.

If you wanted to auction an ATI All-In-Wonder card, for example, it's no great sin to grab the specs and a picture from ATI's Web site. Some people abuse this freedom, however. I've had entire auctions expropriated by others—the product, the graphics, the HTML, the whole shebang. There are scam artists on the Internet just like anywhere else. Keep your antennae up!

Using—and Not Using—Fonts

If you're like me you have lots of groovy fonts. Don't use them! Most people get carried away when they realize how easy HTML is to program with an editor. They jazz up their Web pages with lots of fancy fonts. These fonts won't show up on the Internet, however, unless the viewers of your page have the same fonts installed on their computer. If not, the viewer's Web browser will substitute a default font. If you build your Web pages around fonts everyone has you'll have much better control over how your work appears.

The Universal Fonts

When it comes to fonts the rule of thumb is: variety is the spice of life, but too much spice gives you heartburn! The following fonts are installed on virtually every computer and provide plenty of variety for your ads.

Times New Roman

Courier New

Helvetica

Arial

The first two are called *serif* fonts because they have horizontal or vertical lines, or serifs, at the ends of the strokes. The latter are known as *sans serif* fonts because the ends of the strokes are plain. I mix serif and sans serif fonts, using the former for body text and the latter for headlines.

Another difference you'll note is that every letter in some fonts, such as Courier, takes up the same amount of space on the line. These are known as *fixed pitch* fonts. In the other fonts the letters take only the space required. These variable fonts are called *proportional* fonts and tend to look best in Internet auction ads.

Size Matters

My 19-inch computer monitor displays a whopping 1280×1024 pixels. But my laptop's tiny 10.4-inch screen has a meager 640×480 resolution. Size must be taken into account whenever you create a Web page. The average home monitor is 17 inches, but millions of 14- and 15-inch computer monitors are still in use. And one in three users logs on to the Internet with a laptop computer with an even smaller screen. If you create a Web page with more pixels than will fit onto the average screen, the borders of your page will disappear into the Twilight Zone, the right and bottom margins of the user's Web browser.

Scrolling left and right is not only off-putting, it's a Web design no-no! People are conditioned to scroll up and down a Web page, not left and right. To avoid forcing viewers to do what doesn't come naturally, confine the width of your auction ads to 800 pixels or fewer. If you have a large monitor, try this little test. Reset your display to the following resolutions while viewing a Web page in your Web browser.

➤ 640×480 (Standard 10.4" TFT Laptop or 14" CRT Monitor Resolution known as VGA)

➤ 800×600 (Standard 12" TFT Laptop or 15" CRT Monitor Resolution known as SVGA)

➤ 1024×768 (Standard 14.1"/15" inch TFT Laptop or 17" CRT Monitor Resolution known as XGA)

➤ 1280×1024 (Standard 19" CRT Monitor Resolution known as SXGA)

As you can see, you can fit roughly four VGA screens into one SXGA screen. Since millions of users still surf the Web using VGA and SVGA screens, it's unwise to surpass this boundary. Use the 800-Pixel Table Trick outlined below to make your auction ads the perfect width every time.

HTML Tricks

So far, this chapter has taught you the basics and the secrets of HTML. The only step left is to learn how to apply them. First, here are some tricks to add to your HTML repertoire.

Headline and Font Size

HTML offers six standard headline sizes, 1 through 6. In AOLpress they're on the Format menu under Heading.

HEADING 1 IS 24-POINT TYPE
HEADING 2 IS 18-POINT TYPE
HEADING 3 IS 14-POINT TYPE
HEADING 4 IS 12-POINT TYPE
HEADING 5 IS 10-POINT TYPE
HEADING 6 IS 8-POINT TYPE

In addition, HTML offers seven font sizes, 1 through 7.

FONT 1 IS 8-Point Type

FONT 2 IS 1O-Point Type

FONT 3 IS 12-Point Type (HTML Default)

FONT 4 IS 14-Point Type

FONT 5 IS 18-Point Type

FONT 6 IS 24-Point Type

FONT 7 IS 36-Point Type

To scale your ads proportionately, stick with Heading 1 for headlines and Font Size 2 or 3 for body copy. Font 7 is too large for low-resolution displays and should generally be avoided.

Centering Text

HTML addresses variations in screen size and resolution by centering Web pages automatically in the browser window. This can lead to peculiar-looking or unintentional results. Text and images wrap to the next line, throwing your whole design out of kilter. Look at Figure 7.18—the headlines are identical, only the Web browser widths have changed.

Using an 800-Pixel Table

The easiest way to circumvent the wrapping problem— especially if you have a high-resolution display—is to narrow the window of your HTML editor to 800 pixels using a table as your guide, as shown in Figure 7.19. This is the same trick referred to in "Size Matters," above.

AOLpress doesn't offer a width option in its Table Properties box. There's an 800 Pixel Table on the *Confessions* CD-ROM under Closet Mining Tools. Or if you'd like to try your hand at HTML programming, select Show HTML on the Tools menu in AOLpress and then copy and paste the following text from Chapter 7 on the CD-ROM.

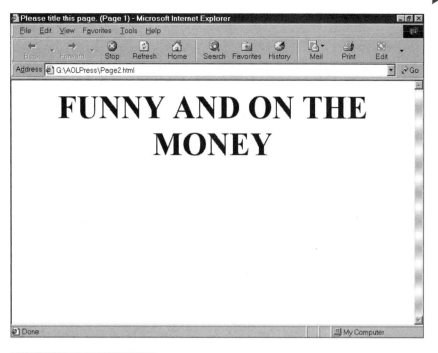

Figure 7.18 *Twin headlines at the mercy of different browser configurations add up to unexpected results.*

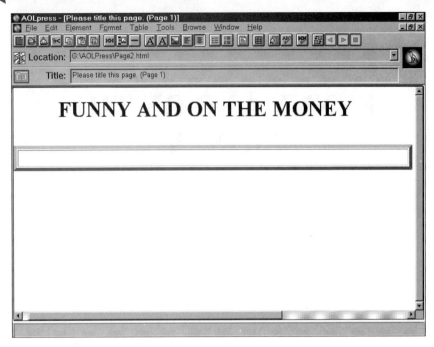

Figure 7.19 *The screen shot was also captured at 800 pixels. That's why it's approximately the same width as the browser window.*

```
<table border="6" cellpadding="3" width="800">
<tr>
<td> </td>
</tr>
</table>
```

Now, size the border of your HTML editor so it matches the approximate width of the table. From now on, when you open the editor its window will default to this width.

Text and images don't wrap in a table the way they do on a Web page. A good technique to make sure people see your ad the way you intended is to use an 800-pixel table to frame your auction ad. Then insert a narrower table within the table to hold the body text, as shown in Figure 7.20. This is not only slick looking; it's an excellent technique to separate images from text and to sectionalize your ads.

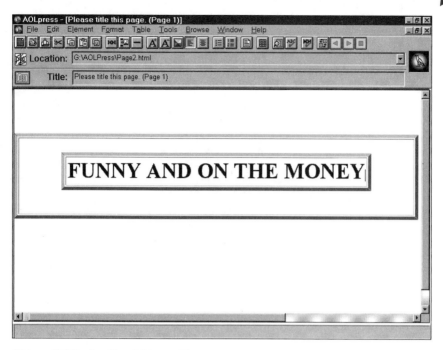

Figure 7.20 *A table within a table*

Sculpting Text

The body copy in my Kit-Cat ad resembles the shape of the clock, as you can see in Figure 7.21.

Sculpting text is neat and creative. The trick is to use a text editor to sculpt the text in pure ASCII first, and then paste the clean text into the HTML editor. To create the same effect in an HTML editor would require laborious editing to remove the <p> (paragraph format code) that HTML editors put at the end of each hard return by default.

I've come to realize that I use a text editor to format text or remove formatting during every HTML session, so I make a habit of opening my text editor every time I open my HTML editor. Get in the habit too!

Background Textures

You can change the background texture of a Web page the same way you change its color. When you right-click in AOLpress, choose the Image option instead of the Color option in the Page Properties box. Figure 7.22 shows a background texture.

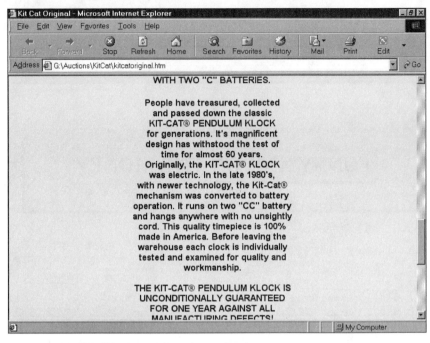

Figure 7.21 *My Kit-Cat ad featuring sculpted text*

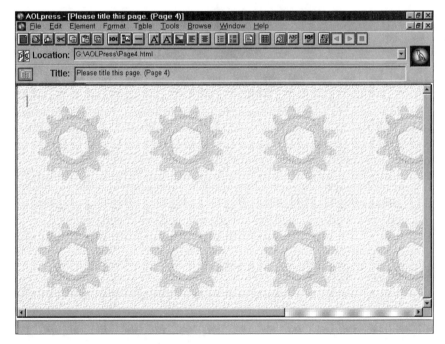

Figure 7.22 *Gears make up the background of this page*

There are thousands of free background GIFs on the Internet, mostly under 5K in size. Click Graphics on the *Confessions* CD-ROM for a generous sampling. You can texture table backgrounds too, but AOLpress doesn't offer this option. To texture a table background in AOLpress, select Show HTML on the Tools menu. Then copy and paste the following text from Chapter 7 on the CD-ROM into AOLpress.

```
<table border="6" cellpadding="3"

BACKGROUND="HTTP://MEMBERS.AOL.COM/URLEGANT/LITEWOOD.GIF">
```

The HTML formula for textured backgrounds is Background=(URL+GIF FILENAME) followed by the cellpadding command. I produced the wood background in Figure 7.23 this way.

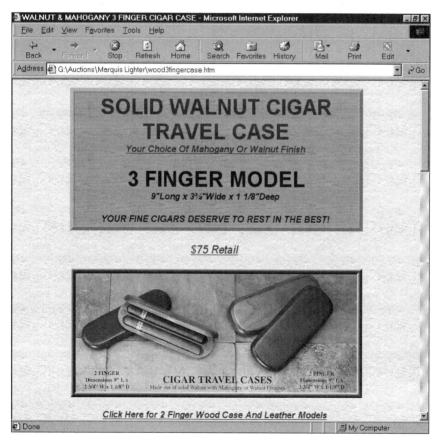

Figure 7.23 *Tables × backgrounds × textures = creativity*

Using Images

A picture of the item you're auctioning is the hallmark of a professional ad. Thanks to bargain scanners, cheap digital cameras, and Photo CDs, obtaining a JPG file of your item is easy. Your options are as follows:

➤ **Photographs**. Any traditional camera will do, even a disposable. Take several pictures of each item at various angles and distances. Get the film developed.

➤ **Scanner**. If you have a scanner, scan the most favorable photo and save it as a JPG file. Restrict the image width to 650 pixels and compress it to under 30K.

➤ **Kodak Photo CD**. When you get your pictures processed ask for a Photo CD if you don't have a scanner. Some ISPs (including AOL) offer Photo CD retrieval on the Web.

➤ **Digital Camera**. You can cut to the chase with a digital camera, which saves pictures in a native JPG format. On high megapixel cameras, shoot at the lowest resolution. Even then you may need to reduce the file size and image width.

➤ **Borrowed Image**. Last but not least, you can borrow a JPG of the item you're auctioning if you can locate one. If the model you're auctioning is current, save the picture from the Web site of the company it came from.

Assignment 11: Get the Picture

Take pictures of the first five items you intend to auction. A scanner is often preferable to a camera when it comes to digitizing images because of the sharp focus and native JPG format. If you use a camera, have fun and be creative! Ask yourself, how would Scavullo or Richard Avedon photograph this? Hint: close-ups work best!

Convert your images into JPG files by any method outlined in the previous list. Create two new folders in your Auction Directory; name one JPG and the other GIF. Give your digital images descriptive file names and save them in the appropriate subdirectory.

Assignment 12: Cut Your Images Down to Size

If you have a scanner, a digital camera, or a graphics and/or office suite, you probably have a decent photo editor. If you don't, click Graphic Programs under Software on the *Confessions* CD-ROM. PaintShop Pro is a popular Windows shareware program that you can try before you buy and ProJPEG is popular for the Mac. Once downloaded and installed, open a JPG file in the editor and resize it by *resampling* the image. I used CorelPaint in the following example.

1. Select the Maintain Aspect Ratio option.
2. Make the image 650 pixels in width or lower. The height will adjust accordingly, as shown in figure 7.24.

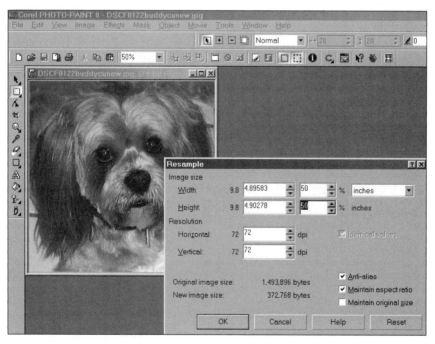

Figure 7.24 *Adjusting the image size by resampling.*

NOTE

When you choose File, Save or File, Save As in many high-end photo editors you're given an option to compress the JPG's disk size by a specified percentage. You can generally compress a JPG file 50 or 60 percent with little visible degradation. Experiment! The smaller the file, the faster your Web page will load.

3. Select Save As, alter the JPG's filename, and compress the JPG to 30K or less by experimenting with the file compression ratio box.

Assignment 13: Continue Closet Mining

Continue to inventory your personal possessions. You'll find things to auction the second time around you never thought of at first glance. Remember, the more you mine you closets, the more moolah will arrive in your mailbox!

Assignment 14: Take Tutorials

There's a wealth of information on the Internet. Take advantage! You can learn more about HTML editing by completing the AOLpress Tutorial. Check out the auction site tutorials by clicking Tutorials under Auction Sites on the *Confessions* CD-ROM. And find even more tutorials on the *Confessions* CD-ROM under Tutorials.

CHAPTER 8

Great Advertising Equals Great Auctions: Let's Light This Candle!

D o you remember Stuart, the disheveled office boy with the Mohawk who teaches his boss, Mr. B., how to trade stocks online in the Ameritrade commercial? It was my favorite TV commercial of the year. What does that commercial have to do with Internet auctions? Great advertising sells, whether it's in a magazine, a TV commercial, or an Internet auction!

The task before you—to create great advertising—is so simple and yet so complex. You now have the tools and knowledge necessary to mine your closet, and an inventory of treasures to auction. You'll be logging much more computer time too, so pop your *Confessions* CD-ROM in your disk drive, open Chapter 8, and as Stuart says, "Let's light this candle!"

Assignment 15: Lose Yourself

It doesn't matter how much time it takes to create your first few auction ads. What matters is how brilliant they are and how well they sell. Get lost in the process. Play around with different color combinations, backgrounds, and text formatting as you brainstorm. Now add an image of the item you're auctioning by inserting its JPG file. You'll be surprised by how creative you are. Sit down in front of the computer, open your HTML editor, and have a blast! Be a maestro, push the envelope. Don't settle for mediocrity—you are an Internet auctioneer!

But first things first—save your work as auction01(product name).htm.

Assignment 16: Swipe This Ad!

Check out my Internet auction ads under Ad Gallery on the *Confessions* CD-ROM for ideas and inspiration. If you see something you like, I invite you to use it. Save the entire page, not just the HTML code, in the Auctions directory on your hard drive. Figure 8.1 illustrates the simple process for saving an ad from the gallery.

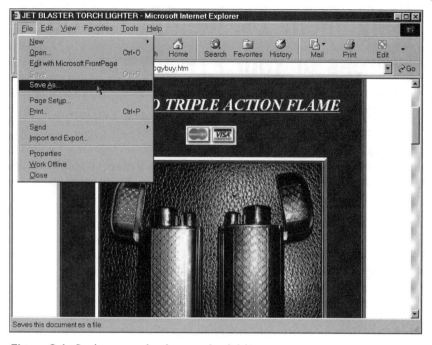

Figure 8.1 *Saving a sample ad to your hard drive*

Feel free to use any of these ads as a template. Open it in your HTML editor and use its table layout, text formatting, or color combination as the basis of your ad. Paste your text and images right over mine. This is a great way to learn HTML! Save the ad as auction02(product name).htm.

Assignment 17: Jazz Up Your Ad

Check out all the punchy and subtle backgrounds available to you on the *Confessions* CD-ROM under Graphics. Save the Complete Web pages, to the CLIPART subdirectory of your Auctions directory. Now do the same with the animated GIFs. The next time you want to jazz up an ad this wealth of clip art will be at your disposal. Visit Barry's Clip Art server link found on the *Confessions* CD-ROM under Graphics when you're online.

Assignment 18: Identify the URL Address of Your FTP Space

While online, find out the URL of your FTP space from your Internet service provider. Obtain detailed instructions on how to upload files to it. Save the instructions in your Auctions\Research directory, and save your URL address in a text file called URLaddress.txt. In the event that your ISP doesn't provide an FTP space there are several auction services that will host your images for free. Click Image Hosting under Services on the *Confessions* CD-ROM for links.

Assignment 19: Search and Rescue

Have you determined the opening bid for the first ten items you're going to auction? If you haven't, the time is ripe to search eBay by brand name, model number, or keyword. If you have determined the opening bid, research the next ten items on your inventory list. Don't forget to search closed auctions in addition to current ones. Search other auction sites, too. Your item may be more in demand on one site than on another. Save your search results in your Auctions\Research folder; don't forget to use descriptive file names!

Assignment 20: Word Play

Log off. Open your word processor—Word, WordPerfect, or whatever—and compose the ad copy for your first Internet auction. Play with your concept and ideas by moving words and sentences around with your mouse. When your wording is tight, copy it to your Clipboard. Paste it into an ASCII text editor to remove all formatting, then copy and paste it in your HTML editor.

Assignment 21: Create a Dazzling Headline

Reinforce your concept with a catchy headline in 45 keystrokes or less. The more outstanding your headline, the more your auction will stand out. Remember that your headline is your bait—write several variations until you hit on one that works. Save it in your Auctions directory in a text file named headlines.txt. Then use your word processor to count characters.

Counting Characters in MS Word

Highlight your headline with your mouse. Select Word Count on the MS Word Tools menu and you'll find your headline's character statistics, both with spaces and without. As you can see in Figure 8.2, the phrase *How to Count a Dazzling 45-Keystroke Headline* is exactly 45 characters (with spaces).

Counting Characters in WordPerfect

Copy and paste your headline into any document and highlight it with your mouse. Select Properties on the File menu and click the Information tab. (The Information area may be in a slightly different location on the File menu depending on the version of WordPerfect you're using, but it's easy to find.) Note that WordPerfect does not include spaces in its count like Word does. The phrase *How to Count a Dazzling 45-Keystroke Headline* contains 39 characters and 6 spaces, which totals 45.

NOTE

If you use WordPerfect, don't forget to tally the spaces and add them to your final character count.

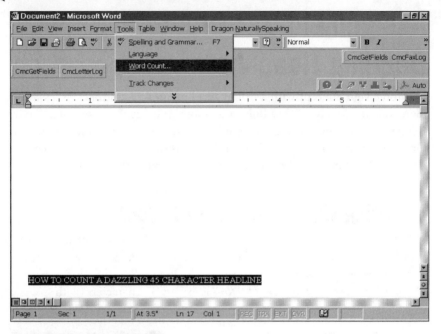

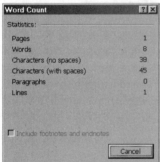

Figure 8.2 *Counting characters in MS Word*

Assignment 22: Picture Perfect

When you're happy with your first ad, it's time to add the finishing touch. Insert the URL address of your JPG and GIF files into your HTML code.

1. Open URLaddress.txt in your text editor. Highlight your URL address with your mouse and copy it.

2. Select the image in your HTML editor.
3. Right-click on it or choose an image on the Element menu.
4. Paste the URL address in the location box directly in front of the name of your image file.

Assignment 23: Calculate Your Costs

Make sure to calculate all of your costs before listing an auction. I once bid on a hundred sheets of inkjet photo stock in a Featured auction by a vendor named Mike. It cost me $18 plus $6 shipping. A few days later the paper arrived by Priority Mail from Florida. The package was hefty—it had cost almost $14 to ship. Poor Mike was obviously losing his shirt! My curiosity got the best of me and I called him to inquire; he related an instructive tale of woe.

Mike's nightmare began when a postal clerk gave him erroneous information about the cost of shipping the paper. Inkjet stock is an Internet auction mainstay that is normally quite lucrative for its vendors. It was a new product for Mike and he was very gung-ho; he invested over a hundred dollars to feature his auction so that it would grab every eye that logged on to eBay's Home page. He underestimated demand—the original auction for 100 packs sold out in days, and Mike listed another Feature auction for 250 packs.

Mike got a bad feeling in the pit of his stomach the moment he began packing the paper. Each package weighed more than the Miami Yellow Pages! His worst suspicions were confirmed the next morning at the post office: instead of $5.30 per package, the shipping cost was $13.82. Mike was taking an $8.52 hit on each order, and he already had over two hundred orders! Mike had anticipated a $6 profit per sale, and instead he was losing $2.52 on each order. Add to that over two hundred dollars he paid to feature his auctions and it turned into a massacre. Mike wound up losing close to $4 per sale and he had to schlep hundreds of bulky packages to the post office for a month.

Calculating Shipping and Handling

Learn from Mike's sad story. Shipping and handling is a double-edged sword. Calculate correctly and you may pocket an extra buck or two. Miscalculations can wipe you out!

> **Rule Number 1**. Never ask a postal employee how much something costs to ship.

> **Rule Number 2**. Measure and weigh the package yourself—then go to http://postcalc.usps.gov/default.asp and calculate the shipping cost yourself.

> **Rule Number 3**. Base the shipping cost on Priority Mail with a delivery confirmation in the continental United States.

> **Rule Number 4**. Consider insurance instead of delivery confirmation so you'll get reimbursed if the USPS loses your package—delivery confirmation doesn't reimburse you.

> **Rule Number 5**. Shipping by Priority Mail provides the benefit of free packaging; remember to factor miscellaneous items you do pay for—such as tape, bubble wrap, and labels—into your shipping fee.

> **Rule Number 6**. Spell out the shipping terms and fee at the bottom of each auction ad—$(dollar amount) for shipping and handling by Priority Mail in the continental United States.

Assignment 24: Uploading JPGs to Your FTP

Open the FTP uploading instructions you saved from your ISP in your Auctions folder. Go online and follow your ISP's instructions step by step. Here are a couple of samples of what the procedure involves, in case you're still getting set up.

1. Type **My FTP Place** in AOL's Address Bar.
2. Click See My FTP Space to view your FTP directory and access the File Manager.
3. Click Upload File.

4. Type (or paste) the name of your JPG file in the file name field box and click Continue.

5. Click Select File and highlight your JPG file in the directory on your hard drive in which it's stored, as shown in Figure 8.3.

6. Click Upload File.

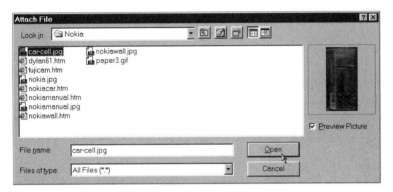

Figure 8.3 *Uploading to AOL*

Assignment 25: Uploading JPG Files in Yahoo! and Amazon

Yahoo! and Amazon host your JPG files on their own Web servers, so you don't have to use your own FTP space. The uploading procedure is similar on each site—see Figure 8.4.

1. On the Sell Item page click the Upload Image button.

2. Highlight your JPG file in the directory in which it's stored on your hard drive.

3. Click Done.

Because of image hosting, listing an auction on Amazon or Yahoo! is somewhat easier than on eBay—but eBay provides maximum exposure and the highest fulfillment rate. The choice is yours. Once you know how to create and list an auction on eBay, doing so on Yahoo! and Amazon is relatively simple. So go ahead and be daring—list your first auction on eBay.

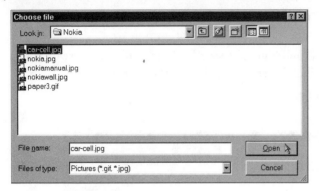

Figure 8.4 *Uploading to Yahoo! and Amazon*

Assignment 25: Do an Integrity Check

View your ad in a Web browser to make sure it looks right after you've uploaded your JPG files to your FTP. View it in both Internet Explorer and Netscape Navigator if you have both. Double-click on your final version of mauction01(product name)x.htm in your file manager while online. If the images appear, list that auction!

Assignment 26: List Your Auction

You just created an Internet auction ad. Congratulations! Have you done your due diligence to come up with a seductive opening bid? Don't price your item too high. Let the bidding take care of that. An opening bid should be low enough to spark competition for your product. In what category are you going to place your auction? Have you conducted searches to discover where people list similar items? How much are you going to charge for shipping? Did you calculate the cost of packaging? Does your ad spell out shipping and handling fees in its text? So far, so good. Listing an auction is a straightforward process. I'll walk you through it, but please don't forget that the auction sites themselves have wonderfully detailed tutorials.

To list your auction on eBay:

1. Double-click on auction1(product name).htm in your File Manager so it opens in your Web browser.
2. Open headlines.txt in your text editor.
3. Open URLaddress.txt in your text editor.
4. Click the eBay logo under Auction Sites on the *Confessions* CD-ROM.
5. Click Sell on eBay's menu bar.
6. Select the main item category by clicking on it.
7. Enter your eBay user ID and password.
8. Highlight your 45-character headline with your mouse in a text editor and copy it to your Clipboard.
9. Paste your headline in eBay's Title field, as shown in Figure 8.5.
10. Select the subcategory in which your item belongs.
11. Right-click on my_auction01(product name).htm in your Web browser and choose View Source, as shown in Figure 8.6.
12. Your text editor will open. Right-click on the HTML code and choose Select All. The source code will be highlighted.
13. Right-click again and choose Copy, as in Figure 8.7. Now paste the source code in eBay's Description field by right-clicking and choosing Paste, as in Figure 8.8.
14. (Optional) Highlight your URL in URLaddress.txt. Copy it and paste it in eBay's Picture URL field.
15. (Optional) Select Add My Item to Gallery.
16. (Optional) Paste your URL address in eBay's Gallery field directly before the name of your JPG file.

NOTE

Adding your JPG image to the gallery increases your exposure. Besides, what else can you buy for a quarter?

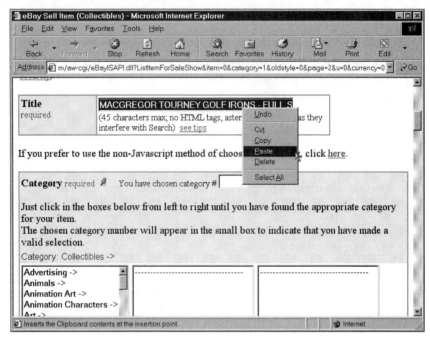

Figure 8.5 *Pasting your headline*

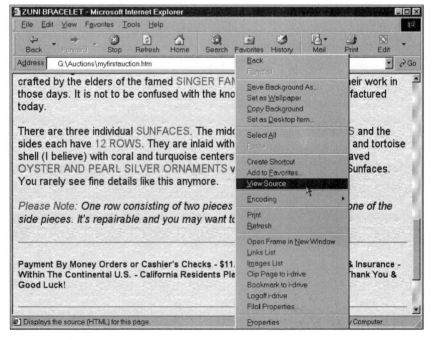

Figure 8.6 *Getting ready to grab your code*

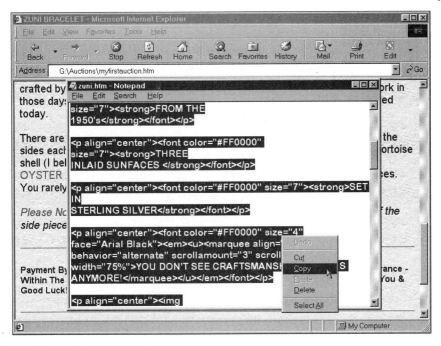

Figure 8.7 *Copy your code. . . .*

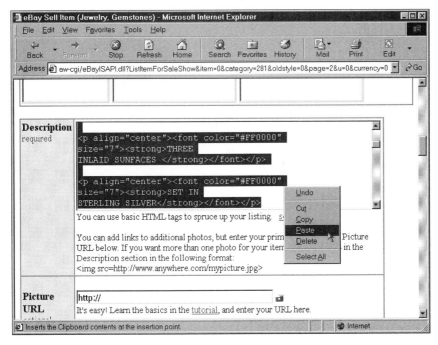

Figure 8.8 *And paste it into your ad.*

17. Skip down to Item Location and fill in your location.

18. In Payment Method, select Money Order/Cashier's Check and Personal Check.

19. (Optional) Choose whether to accept payment by escrow.

20. In Where Will You Ship, select United States Only to keep things simple. Of course, if you live in another country and/or want to ship internationally, be my guest.

21. In Who Pays for Shipping, select Buyer Pays Fixed Amount and See Item Description.

22. Fill in the Quantity.

23. Fill in your Minimum Bid. Make it low enough!

24. Select a Duration of 7 days, the optimum length for your closet mining auctions.

25. Click Review.

Review the next page carefully. If everything checks out, click Submit. That's all there is to it. You're on your own now; take off the training wheels and fly! Mine every nugget in your closet until there's nothing left.

If a reasonable facsimile of your auction doesn't appear, repeat Steps 8 through 11 in the preceding exercise. Hit your Web browser's Back button. Clear eBay's Description field by right-clicking, choose Select All, and then hit Backspace on your keyboard. Copy your HTML code from your text editor again and paste it into eBay's empty Description field.

If you encounter Web browser errors while listing an auction using Internet Explorer, use Netscape Navigator instead.

Whatever happens, don't panic! Learn from your mistakes. Turn them into opportunities. Trace your problem to its root by reviewing Chapters 7 and 8 as well as the auction site tutorials.

CHAPTER 9

Surviving the Digital Blitzkrieg: Switching Hats and Selling Kit-Cats

> The Successful Internet Auction 12-Step Program

> Word Processor Database

> Managing E-Mail Like a Pro

> Using Auction Software

> Assignment 27: Mine Your Own Business

> Assignment 28: Track Your Auctions with Your Home Page

- ➤ **Seventh Step**. E-mail the winner a thank-you acknowledgment for his or her payment.

- ➤ **Eighth Step**. Deposit payment in your bank immediately. If it's a personal check, it can take several business days to clear. Ask your bank to explain their hold policy.

- ➤ **Ninth Step**. Pack the item neatly and securely in free boxes you get at the post office. Include a copy of the invoice, marked *paid*.

- ➤ **Tenth Step**. Ship the item in a timely manner. You must mail it from a post office to get insurance or delivery confirmation.

- ➤ **Eleventh Step**. Post positive feedback for the winner.

- ➤ **Twelfth Step**. E-mail the winner that the item has shipped and that you have posted positive feedback. Request positive feedback in return.

Congratulations! You've completed the program. Eighteen hats and twelve steps, that's what an Internet auctioneer juggles. Once you set up your software to exchange information, the tasks themselves become second nature. Interchange is accomplished primarily via the computer Clipboard by copying and pasting information between interrelated databases in your word processor, PIM or contact manager, and e-mail manager.

Using a Word Processor Database

Which word processor you use doesn't matter. How you use it does. A form mail database includes form letters that you customize for each winning auction stored in your word processor. Every form letter is preceded by a unique header that includes the auction's close date, headline, item number, and winner's e-mail address.

NOTE

In the upcoming examples, underlined characters are specific to each particular auction; other characters are constant.

At a minimum you'll require three form letters: Winner's Notice, Order Processed, and Item Shipped. Form mail should be polite and convey information precisely.

The Winner's Notice

The Winner's Notice is most crucial because it covers the most ground. Feel free to adapt mine from the sample given here. (As noted, the underlined fields reflect the specifics of the auction; plug in the equivalent data from your own auction.)

Sample Header:

March 7, 2000 (The Auction's Close Date Changes)

SEAFOAM KIT-CAT CLOCK 1999 LIMITED EDITION - V/MC (Item #270181960) (Headline and Item Number Changes)

XXXetick@frontiernet.net (The Auction Winner Changes)

Winner's Notice:

Congratulations!

You won eBay auction #270181960 for the Seafoam Kit-Cat. Thank you for bidding. Your order comes to $42.49 (includes S&H in continental U.S. – Outside continental U.S. please contact me for revised shipping).

Credit Card Payments

Point your Web Browser to:

http://members.aol.com/urlegant/default.htm

Click on Let the Shopping Begin and you'll be whisked to The Kit-Cat Shopping Cart. Place your order and click Proceed to Secure Server on the Check Out page.

PAYMENT BY CHECK OR MONEY ORDER

Please send your payment in the amount of $42.49 (includes S&H in Continental U.S. – Outside Continental U.S. please contact me for revised shipping) to:

Michael Weber

XXX Kings Road

Beverly Hills, CA 90069

Remember to include your full name and mailing address. California residents please add 8.25% sales tax. Orders paid by money order or cashier's check are processed immediately. Orders paid by personal check are processed upon clearance. Please e-mail me at your earliest convenience to acknowledge you received this -- and thanks again for bidding.

Have a great day!

Michael

A Winner's Notice is essentially an invoice. It includes:

➤ The auction site name

➤ The auction number

➤ The name of the item

➤ The price

➤ The payment terms

➤ The payment request

➤ The payment instructions

➤ The shipping address

➤ The shipping terms

➤ A thank you

Create a new Winner's Notice for each winning auction. Here's a Winner's Notice customized for a different auction.

March 7, 2000

Marquis Dunhill Lookalike Butane Lighter V/MC (Item #270171012)

XXXheek@bellsouth.net

Congratulations!

You won eBay auction # XXX171012 for the Marquis Butane Lighter. Thank you for bidding. Your order comes to $36.99 (includes S&H in Continental U.S. – Outside Continental U.S. please contact me for revised shipping).

Credit Card Payments

Point your Browser to the following Web Page and order the blue or black Marquis by clicking either Buy-It! button:

http://members.aol.com/urlegant/marquisbuy.htm

PAYMENT BY CHECK OR MONEY ORDER

Please send your payment in the amount of $36.99 (includes S&H in Continental U.S. – Outside Continental U.S. please contact me for revised shipping) to:

Michael Weber

XXX Kings Road

Beverly Hills, CA 90069

Remember to include your full name and mailing address. California residents please add 8.25% sales tax. Orders paid by money order or cashier's check are processed immediately. Orders paid by personal check are processed upon clearance. Please e-mail me at your earliest convenience to acknowledge you received this -- and thanks again for bidding.

Have a great day!

Michael

Create a new form mail database every month. Save the file as Auction Winners (January).xxx, Auction Winners (February).xxx, etc., in your word processor. This will simplify searches and keep the file size manageable.

The Order Processed and Item Shipped Notices

In addition to the Winner's Notice, add two other forms: Order Processed and Item Shipped to your database. These forms are generic and require no changes except for the header.

Order Processed:

> *XXXram@home.com, XXXviccyc@aol.com, XXXtav58@aol.com, XXXordpr@aol.com, XXXbeth@aol.com, XXXmomjk@aol.com*
>
> *March 9, 2000*
>
> *Order Processed*
>
> *Greetings,*
>
> *Thanks for your payment. Your order has been processed.*
>
> *Michael*

Item Shipped:

> *March 14, 2000*
>
> *XXXmedbybskts@aol.com, XXX@bobsliberace.com, XXXumka@aol.com, XXXrschg@csj.net, XXXlmcc@ncool.net*
>
> *Greetings,*
>
> *Your order has shipped. I posted positive feedback for you on eBay and when the order arrives I'd appreciate the same.*
>
> *Thanks again!*
>
> *Michael*

If you ship the order when you receive payment, you can combine the Order Processed and Item Shipped notices.

> *Greetings,*
>
> *Thanks for your payment. Your order has shipped. I posted positive feedback for you on eBay and when the order arrives I'd appreciate the same.*
>
> *Thanks again!*
>
> *Michael*

Add to your form mail database accordingly. Use any information you find yourself repeating as a template for subsequent form e-mail.

Managing E-Mail Like a Pro

Respond to all e-mail promptly! A response may be as short as a phrase or a sentence. Time is of the essence. Parse longer e-mail in your word processor for spelling errors. Always be respectful and polite!

Opening a New E-Mail Account

Establish a new e-mail account strictly for your Internet auctions and don't intermingle it with your other e-mail. If your ISP doesn't offer multiple e-mail accounts, sign up with an e-mail portal such as Hotmail, Deja Mail, or Yahoo! Mail. Create a short descriptive e-mail name that corresponds to your auction handle.

Keeping an E-Mail Database

Save all e-mail pertaining to your auctions, even the most inconsequential. You may need it as a reference someday. I've had winners not receive packages because they accidentally transposed their shipping address in their e-mail. In such a case, having a buyer's e-mail handy as evidence that you were on the ball can save your reputation. I couldn't have written this book without the material in my e-mail archive (Figure 9.1).

Refer to your e-mail manager for instructions on archiving e-mail.

Figure 9.1 *Deleting your e-mail transactions can come back to haunt you.*

Using Batch E-Mail

Batch e-mail enables you to send duplicate copies of a message to several people at the same time, as in the Item Shipped example (mentioned earlier, and shown in Figure 9.2). Unfortunately, batch e-mail is at the root of all spam—junk e-mail—as well. Batch e-mail is a marvelous convenience that should be taken advantage of whenever the opportunity presents itself. . . but don't make a nuisance of yourself!

Using a PIM

First name, last name, address, city, ZIP code, e-mail address, phone number, auction date, auction number, invoice number, item purchased, amount— every winner who pays you has one of each. PIMs archive personal information in a database dedicated to this undertaking. A personal information manager (or *contact manager* as they're sometimes called) is the centerpiece of your Internet auction toolbox. Outlook, Act, Goldmine, and Corel Central are popular commercial PIMs.

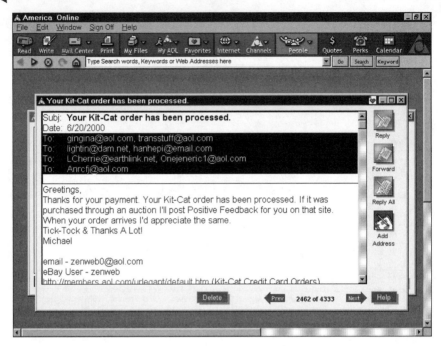

Figure 9.2 *Batch e-mail in action*

I happen to use Commence, a highly customizable PIM that I adapted specifically to track Internet auctions—see Figures 9.3 and 9.4. Which PIM you use doesn't matter. What does matter is the ability to copy and paste information from your other databases into the PIM's data fields via the Clipboard. Most PIMs support this feature. If you don't have one, download a shareware PIM by following the links under Software on the *Confessions* CD-ROM.

As an alternative to a full-blown PIM, look no further than your word processor. Word and WordPerfect have more than adequate address book capabilities and using them can integrate two databases into a single program. Refer to your word processor for detailed instructions.

➤ In Word, click Envelopes and Labels on the Tools menu.

➤ In WordPerfect, click Address Book on the Tools menu.

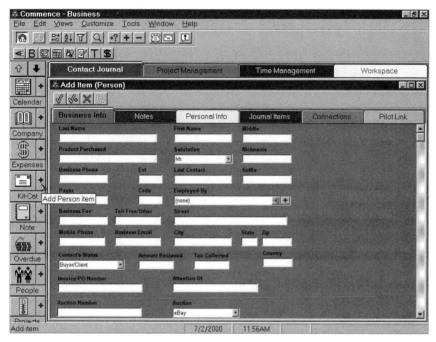

Figure 9.3 *Commence input form*

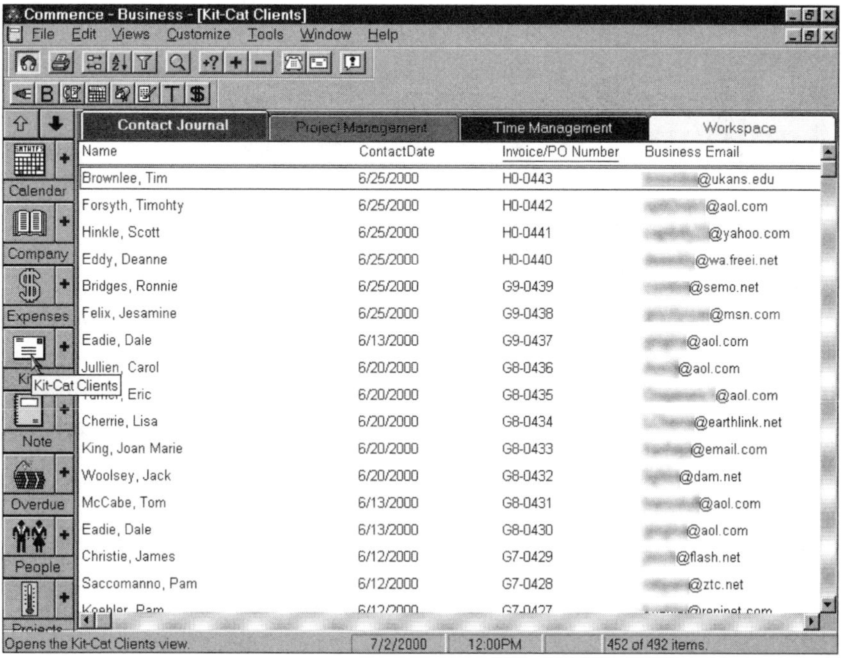

Figure 9.4 *Name, date, Invoice/PO number, e-mail address, model: a list of my Kit-Cat clients in Commence*

Using Auction Software

The burgeoning popularity of Internet auctions has spawned a cottage software industry. Hundreds of Internet auction programs have hit the market recently and some are quite commendable; others are more bother than they're worth. All have a learning curve. The best of these programs do nothing more than what you're learning to do with software you already own. You may find the specialized nature of these programs appealing, however. Auction software breaks down into three basic categories.

> ➤ **Auction Managers** track auction data and schedules.
> ➤ **Auction Designers** generate templates and HTML ads.
> ➤ **Auction Bots** search multiple auction sites.

I haven't had an opportunity to evaluate them in detail, but you'll find links to several auction utilities under Software on the *Confessions* CD-ROM.

These programs are shareware and cost between $30 and $50 to purchase. The trial versions have limited functionality and expire after a designated amount of time. Frankly, these auction utilities remind me of screenwriting software. For the life of me I never understood why people spent hard-earned money on such software when they could format a screenplay just as easily with the word processor they already own.

Assignment 27: Mine Your Own Business

Continually create new auctions until you liquidate your entire inventory. Mine your closets over and over again. You have a much better idea of what to look for now. Try different auction sites and techniques. Do any of your items lend themselves to Reserve Price auctions? Relist items that don't sell the first time. Rethink your strategy. The headline, opening bid, or category in which you placed the item are the most likely culprits when an auction fails.

Assignment 28: Track Your Auctions with Your Home Page

You can make any page on the Internet your home page by specifying its URL as your Web browser's default. Once you're an auctioneer, you may as well have the thing you're most interested in—the money you're making from your stuff—show up first when you start your Web browser.

My home page tracks the status of my auctions on eBay; Figure 9.5 shows a small section as a sample.

If you'd like to try this, click View Seller's Other Auctions in any of *your* auctions. Then copy and paste the resulting URL in the Default Home Page Address field of your Web browser, as shown in Figure 9.6.

Item	Start	End	Price	Title	High Bidder
366426556	Jun-24-00	Jul-04-00 09:53:13	$33.99	FELIX THE KIT-CAT CLOCK ORIGINAL CLASSIC V/MC	0 Dutch bids
366425961	Jun-24-00	Jul-04-00 09:52:08	$33.99	FELIX THE KIT-CAT CLOCK ORIGINAL CLASSIC V/MC	2 Dutch bids
366424709	Jun-24-00	Jul-04-00 09:49:46	$38.99	CHROME KIT-CAT CLOCK MILLENNIUM EDITION V/MC	2 Dutch bids
366423417	Jun-24-00	Jul-04-00 09:48:00	$48.99	HAND JEWELED LTD EDITION KIT-CAT CLOCK - V/MC	4 Dutch bids
366422473	Jun-24-00	Jul-04-00 09:45:30	$35.99	SEAFOAM KIT-CAT CLOCK 1999 LIMIT EDITION V/MC	1 Dutch bids
366421696	Jun-24-00	Jul-04-00 09:43:58	$35.99	LILAC KIT-CAT CLOCK 1999 LIMITED EDITION V/MC	0 Dutch bids
366420860	Jun-24-00	Jul-04-00 09:42:10	$33.99	FELIX THE KIT-CAT CLOCK ORIGINAL CLASSIC V/MC	4 Dutch bids

Figure 9.5 *My home page displays the current status of my auctions.*

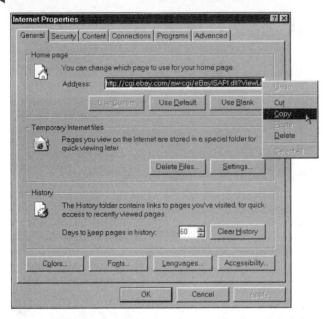

Figure 9.6 *How I made my Internet auctions my default home page in Internet Explorer*

Your PC as an Internet Auction Assembly Line: Factory or Fiction?

> Shifting for Yourself

> Go into a Trance and Dance

t was the middle of the gas crisis; I had just moved to L.A. and needed a car. I fell head-over-heels for a little Honda Accord. The only problem was that it came with a manual transmission—Honda didn't make an automatic that year. I didn't know how to drive a stick shift but I bought it anyway. While my car was on back order I rented a Pinto with a stick shift and my friend Judy taught me how to shift gears. We began by stalling in empty parking lots and worked our way onto the Hollywood Freeway. By the time I took possession of that Honda I was shifting gears in my sleep!

Just like me with my Honda, you must learn to shift gears in your sleep with your Internet auction tools—the various software programs that you will come to rely on to make you an efficient Internet auctioneer.

Shifting for Yourself

Windows, the Mac OS, and Linux were all designed from the bottom up to be multitasking environments. They allow data to be transferred between programs. Those little icons on the Windows taskbar represent open programs between which you can transfer data. There's no better way to manage Internet auctions than to multitask. In fact, by the time you finish mining your closet, you'll be a multitasking maven!

Chapter 9 defines Internet auction software, introduces it in theory, and helps you set up your computer. This chapter challenges you to put what you've learned into practice. You have the necessary tools: a word processor, PIM, and an e-mail manager. The next example demonstrates how to use the tools when you have a winning auction.

Step 1: You Have a Winner!

It's your responsibility to check your auctions when they close. The auction site will send you e-mail—but auction sites are notoriously late when it comes to notifying people. It typically takes eBay eight to 16 hours to e-mail an official notification, so you're already dealing with an impatient winner by the time you hear from the site. Make sure you jump on the notice quickly when it arrives.

It's worth studying this type of e-mail notice in detail. The underlined items in the notice that follows (from a different auction, not from that in Figure 10.1) are the ones that form the foundation for an auction database. First, save the winner's e-mail address plus the auction headline and number in your e-mail address book.

> *Dear zenweb and <u>XXXumka@aol.com</u>*
>
> *Congratulations -- this auction successfully ended.*
>
> *Item Title: <u>WHITE KIT-CAT KLOCK -- RARE ONE OF A KIND V/MC (Item #269210458)</u>*
>
> *Final price:*   <u>*$60.00*</u>
>
> *Auction ended at:*   *Mar-05-00 19:09:24 PST*
>
> *Total number of bids:*   <u>*1*</u>
>
> *Seller User ID:*   *zenweb*
>
> *Seller E-mail:*   *zenweb0@aol.com*
>
> *High-bidder User ID:*   <u>*XXXumka@aol.com*</u>
>
> *High-bidder E-mail:*   <u>*XXXumka@aol.com*</u>

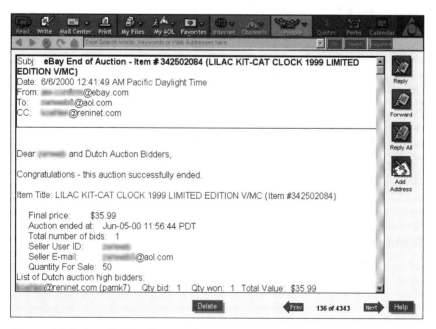

Figure 10.1 *It took eBay almost 13 hours to e-mail this End Of Auction notification.*

Figure 10.2 shows this operation in progress. This information makes up the header of your winner's notice. Open your word processor and copy the information from your e-mail address book to your form mail database, then time-stamp it.

March 6, 2000

WHITE KIT-CAT KLOCK -- RARE ONE OF A KIND V/MC (Item #269210458)

XXXumka@aol.com

Next, customize the Winner's Notice form by pasting the relevant data into the corresponding fields. Notice I added the shipping cost ($6.50) to the auction price ($60).

> *Congratulations XXXumka@aol.com!*
>
> *You won eBay auction #269210458 for the WHITE KIT-CAT KLOCK. Thank you for bidding. Your order comes to $66.50 (includes S&H in CONTINENTAL U.S. -- Outside CONTINENTAL U.S. please contact me for revised shipping).*

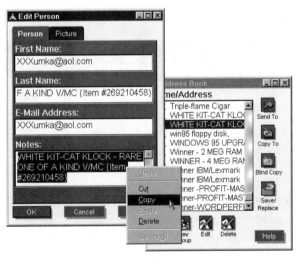

Figure 10.2 *Setting up an auction address book entry*

Step 2: E-mail the Winner's Notice

Save your updated form mail database and e-mail the customized Winner's Notice and payment instructions to the winner. The winner received e-mail notification from the auction site at the same time that you did, so be prompt.

Congratulations XXXumka@aol.com!

You won eBay auction #269210458 for the WHITE KIT-CAT KLOCK. Thank you for bidding. Your order comes to $66.50 (includes S&H in CONTINENTAL U.S. -- Outside CONTINENTAL U.S. please contact me for revised shipping) Please send your payment in the amount of $66.50 (includes S&H in CONTINENTAL U.S. -- Outside CONTINENTAL U.S. please contact me for revised shipping) to:

Michael Weber

xxx Kings Road

Beverly Hills, CA 90069

Remember to include your FULL NAME AND MAILING ADDRESS. CALIFORNIA RESIDENTS PLEASE ADD 8.25% SALES TAX. Orders paid by money order or cashier's check are processed immediately. Orders paid by personal check are processed upon clearance. Please e-mail me at your earliest convenience to acknowledge you received this and thanks again for bidding.

Have a great day!

Michael

Step 3: Digitize and Dispose When Payment Arrives

If both parties are on the ball, there's an intermediate step between Step 2 and Step 3. A courteous bidder sends an e-mail note to the auctioneer when the payment goes into the mail, and an attentive auctioneer immediately replies with a thank-you note. This reassures both sides that the deal is on track.

The real work starts when the payment arrives with the shipping info. The first thing to do is open your PIM and digitize the winner's shipping info and the auction details, as shown in Figure 10.3. The next thing is to dispose of the paper in which the payment arrived. I shred and recycle mine. If you don't do this regularly, a mountain of useless envelopes and letters will quickly pile up.

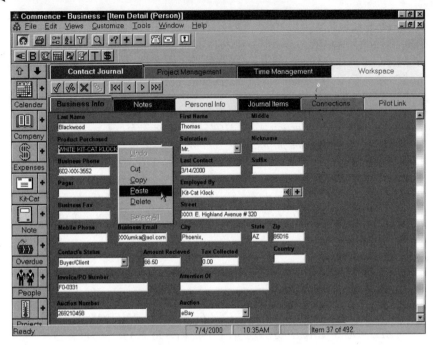

Figure 10.3 *Filling out the PIM*

All contact managers and personal information managers have fields for first name, last name, e-mail address, street address, city, state, ZIP code, and phone. I find it useful to catalog the date, item name, number, auction site, and the amount and type of payment, in addition to the basics. Once you digitize the vital statistics of the transaction you can dispose of all the paper associated with it—envelopes, letters—whatever—with total peace of mind.

Here's another rule of thumb: never type what you can paste! It's far easier to copy and paste data than to key it in. It's also more accurate and reliable. Check your e-mail database for correspondence with the winner. Most winners include their name and address in their initial e-mail. If this is the case, copy and paste the data into your PIM, as shown in Figure 10.4.

Step 4: Bank and Pack

Deposit the payment ASAP. Then pack the item. When it comes to packing, remember that the item is no longer yours; give it a proper send-off! Clean it up and pack it with care in the free Priority Mail box you got at the post office. Invest in some bubble wrap to protect the item in transit.

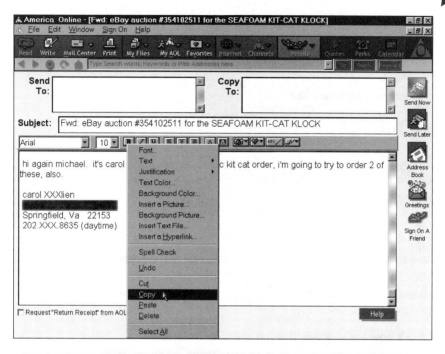

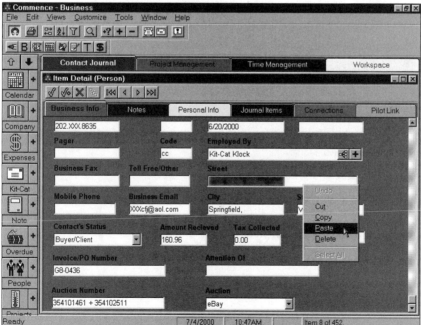

Figure 10.4 *Grabbing an address from e-mail*

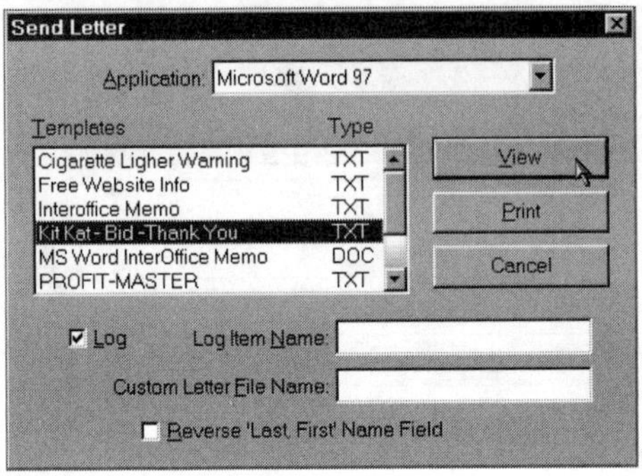

Figure 10.6 *Triggering a thank-you note*

A thank-you note is optional but adds a touch of class. Your word processor and PIM allow you to create form letters by extrapolating fields from your address book and merging them with fields in a form letter. Figure 10.6 shows how my system works. Refer to your word processor or PIM for detailed instructions.

Here's how the code for this letter looks:

(-Date-)

(%Salutation%) (%First Name%) (%Last Name%)

(%PrimaryAddress%)

(%PrimCity%) (%PrimState%) (%PrimZip%)

INVOICE:(%Invoice/PO Number%)

Dear (%First Name%),

Here's your new (%Product Purchased%). It was a pleasure doing business with you.

Tick-Tock & Thanks A Lot!

The fields in parentheses were extrapolated by my PIM resulting in the following form thank-you note. The other characters comprise the text of the message which remains constant. Here's the result:

March 30, 2000

Mr. Craig XXXee

XXX4 NW 189th Way #12

Beaverton, OR 976xx

INVOICE: F3-0649

Dear Craig,

Here's your <u>CHROME MILLENNIUM EDITION KIT-CAT KLOCK</u>. It was a pleasure doing business with you.

Tick-Tock & Thanks A Lot!

Step 5: The Trip to Ship

The form of payment dictates when to ship. Having processed several hundred personal checks I find it remarkable and reassuring that not one has ever bounced! I'd like to tell you I always err on the side of caution and wait five business days for personal checks to clear, but it wouldn't be true. On the other hand, there's no rush. When mining your closet, you'll have several auctions running at once. You can consolidate trips to the post office by shipping multiple items at the same time when they've been paid for by personal check.

The rules change when you're paid by money order. Pack the item immediately and ship it within twenty-four hours. Then deposit the payment. Money orders are good!

Step 6: Provide Closure

Leave positive feedback for the winner and e-mail your form Shipping Notice. Don't forget to request positive feedback! Here's the notice I use:

Greetings,

Thanks for your payment. Your Kit-Cat order has been processed. I posted positive feedback for you on eBay and when the order arrives I'd appreciate the same.

Tick-Tock & Thanks A Lot!

Go into a Trance and Dance

Are you still with me? I promised I'd explain the arcane and make the mundane palatable and I assure you Steps 1 through 6 are easier to execute than read about. Once you set up the proper databases and forms, managing all of these details merely involves a bunch of copying and pasting.

Turn your computer into an Internet auction assembly line! Put on your favorite music CD, go into a trance, and dance between databases. Copy, paste; paste, copy, get in the groove. It's like shifting gears. Pretty soon you'll be able to do it in your sleep!

CHAPTER 11

Avoiding the Pitfalls of Success: Take a Deep Breath and Count to Ten

There is no success like failure and failure is no success at all. . . .

--Bob Dylan

Were you surprised that there were no assignments at the end of the last chapter? You're on your own now! How many auctions do you currently have running? When you're closet mining, three or four a week—one auction every other day or so—is a good pace. Did you have any winners yet? Greenbacks rolling into your mailbox will start to add up. Depending on how many auctions you list, hundreds if not thousands of dollars will filter into your bank account. It soon becomes apparent that these aren't mere transactions. They're real relationships with people to whom you're passing on your belongings. It's personal!

Internet auctions have provided me the best geography lesson I've had since high school. Clackamas (Oregon), Albemarle (North Carolina), Oconto Falls (Wisconsin), Mundelein (Illinois), Galena (Missouri)—I know people in these places because their envelopes found their way into my mailbox, as you can see in Figure 11.1.

Here are a few sample e-mails:

> ➤ *Thanks for responding so quickly! I'm purchasing it for my father's 76th birthday. He has wanted one for 35 years (that I can remember) but my mother would never let him have one. She finally relented and told me if I see one at an auction or estate sale to get it. He will be thrilled!*

> ➤ *I've bought several Kit-Cat clocks from you, a couple of which I gave to our local Humane Society for their new shelter. People have been interested in the one in the lobby, and I would like to get a few to give them that they can sell to the public for raising funds.*

> ➤ *I wonder if you can cancel my bid? This was a gift for my sister. Yesterday she had to put her cat to sleep due to leukemia, and I'm afraid that this would not be a good memory right now. I am truly sorry.*

> ➤ *A friend of mine eventually wants to buy a Kit-Cat Clock. She's waiting for her income tax return. I'm going to tell her about yours. I bought one from you and it runs like a Maytag.*

Figure 11.1 *Friends from faraway places*

> ➤ *I have great memories of my Aunt Ever's Kit Cat clock with the jeweled eyes. I know this one is new, but it already has sentimental value.*

> ➤ *Please accept our apologies. Our son is deceased. Please remove the bid. We have left positive feedback for all those he left bids with. Again, sorry.*

I once received an envelope addressed in a scrawl so illegible that I was surprised the post office could deliver it. The postmark was Norman, Oklahoma. The note inside was equally indecipherable, but I deduced from the printing on the check and my databases that it was from a fellow named Ed in payment for a black Marquis lighter. I processed the order and thought nothing more of it until another envelope arrived the following week written in the same illegible scrawl. I immediately recognized the handwriting as Ed's. I figured it was a mistake and e-mailed him. Ed e-mailed me back that he wanted another lighter so I sent him one.

When a third check arrived from Ed, only days later, I grew apprehensive. I've unhappily witnessed the ravages of Alzheimer's disease and had a hunch that's what I was dealing with. I stuffed the uncashed check in an envelope and mailed it back to Ed.

A couple of weeks passed and I began to notice an awful lot of winning bids coming from—you guessed it—Norman, Oklahoma. Kit-Cat clocks, cigarette lighters, humidors. It appeared different folks from Norman were gobbling up every item I auctioned. Now I ask you, how big is Norman, Oklahoma? I got the distinct impression that I had a fan club there, a geriatric gang of pranksters sitting on a porch, laughing—but not at my expense. They gave me hundreds of dollars worth of business!

I just want Ed and his pals from Norman to know that I'm on to them, I thank them, and hope that they buy this book.

Letters, We Get Letters

We get lots and lots of letters! Each is a story. It's easy to lose sight of that when the letters start piling up because you're running so many auctions. You've got to photograph items, create ads, upload JPGs, list auctions, answer e-mail, keep accurate records, pack, ship, bank, and on top of all that, you're supposed to be a diplomat? You bet! Above all else you must be a good *netizen,* a good citizen of the Internet. Afford others the dignity and respect they deserve!

People Will Be People

Of course, it's not always that simple. People will be people, and among your transactions you'll encounter people who are difficult, annoying, and overly demanding.

Of all my Internet auction customers, LoveDove@XXX.com (e-mail address changed to protect user's privacy) was the biggest nightmare; the painful truth is that I was at fault. I was running a Dutch auction for hand-jeweled French Lilac Kit-Cat clocks. It was an exceptionally rare item, a double Limited Edition; I was under the impression the warehouse had plenty, but I was wrong. By the time my auction closed there were barely enough left in stock to satisfy my eight bidders. The warehouse put them on hold.

I spelled out the situation clearly in my e-mail and seven of the eight bidders responded by sending payment within a week. LoveDove was the only holdout. It was just as well—the warehouse tests each clock before they ship to make sure they work, and they found a dud! Then, ten days later, LoveDove e-mailed me.

I bought the money order for the French Lilac Jeweled Kit-Cat Klock, and was about to mail it, when I realized I never got your snail address. I would appreciate it so I can get this out. Purrs, LoveDove

Of course I included my "snail address" in my form Winner's Notice, but that was irrelevant. I now had to fess up to LoveDove.

I'm afraid there are no more Lilac Jeweled models left. They all sold out. I'd recommend getting a black jeweled, while they last, or a lilac without jewels. Sorry about the lilac jeweled, but as you know the stock was limited.

To put it mildly, LoveDove gave me a piece of her mind.

That's a really dumb explanation! I asked for a lilac, and was told by you I was saved one. You never said it was to be doled out 1st come, 1st serve (or I would've overnighted the money). Then, you as a responsible seller, were supposed to hold that exact lilac colored item that I was promised to me for me and sell only the others. That's how it works in business. I am aghast at this irresponsibility. BTW, I was informed I had won on 10/11. That was only 10 days ago. All sellers are required by e-Bay to hold items for 10 days before reselling or re-listing it. You obviously didn't. You didn't warn me you were running out. You obviously didn't care at all about my individual purchase. That is poor business practice. BTW, I don't want a black one. I hate black clocks. I collect purple cats! I am also disabled and was very much looking forward to this brightening my home. I expect you to try to find one for me as promised. If not, I shall have to make a complaint to e-Bay. I do not want to, but this is ridiculous!

I don't like to get too down on myself, but she was right. I deplored her tone, however! It ticked me off. I took a deep breath and counted to ten, then called Arthur and Eileen, the clock's manufacturers, to explain my dilemma. They were most understanding and promised to call around to locate another jeweled lilac model. In the meantime, I e-mailed LoveDove.

I put a call into the manufacturer. I'll let you know when they locate one.

True to their word, Arthur and Eileen called a few days later with good news. They unearthed a jeweled lilac for me. I was ecstatic! I e-mailed LoveDove.

On your behalf I've located what is likely the last Lilac Jeweled Kit-Cat Klock in the world. Please forward your money order ASAP.

LoveDove e-mailed me her kudos.

> *THANK YOU SOOOOO MUCH! I will give you a fab rating, believe me. You made my week! Okay, the M.O. was made out for $51.00, b/c clock was $47.50 and I never found out how much the shipping was. If it is $6.50 more (please advise) I will gladly add 3 one's in the envelope, which I shall have hubby mail out tomorrow. You will have the $ ASAP. If I don't hear from you, I'll just send the $51+$3. It's not the $ I care about! It's the clock! I am so happy!*

Frankly, I didn't care about the money either. I just wanted closure. During this Transaction from Hell I'd exchanged over 30 e-mails in the course of three weeks. Those included here are only the highlights and lowlights.

Another week passed. No payment. Arthur and Eileen called. Several other customers would be happy to take the lilac jeweled Kit-Cat clock if I was having a problem. I told them to hold off and e-mailed LoveDove to inquire about the status of her payment. Sometimes I'm too stubborn for my own good, as you can see. LoveDove responded.

> *Payment for the lilac jeweled Kit Kat Klock was mailed last Monday. I bet it'll be there today. I will pray! You know how much I appreciate this!*

I got down on my hands and knees and prayed with her, a first and a last! The payment finally arrived, three dollars short, twenty-eight days later. The last time I heard from LoveDove was after her clock arrived. She e-mailed me.

> *Thanks! I swear this will be one of my most favorite and memorable purchases on e-Bay ever! Will leave you smashing feedback:)*

Do you think she left me smashing feedback, or any feedback at all? No! All she left me was bruised and abused. The point of the tale? On the Internet there's no room to lose your temper. In real life I don't suffer fools gladly. I've even been accused of being confrontational. But when I go on the Internet, I leave my attitude at home. I try to be a good netizen.

Had I not been partially responsible, I would have elected not to participate in this protracted transaction. Lovedove was obviously more trouble than she was worth. I treated her with dignity and respect, and though she didn't respond in kind, I'm proud of myself for doing so. There is one particular upon which LoveDove and I are in total accord. This *is* my most memorable Internet auction transaction too!

Dealing with Crunch Time

When you're running three or four auctions a week, there'll come a time you're so inundated by minutiae that you want to pull a blanket over your head and chuck it. The redundancy gets to you. You feel like Bill Murray in the movie *Groundhog Day*. You've made so many round trips to the bank and post office that you not only know the clerks and tellers by their first name, you know the names of their children. You get stuck in traffic, the Internet is painfully slow, and your Web browser crashes at all the wrong times.

Take a deep breath and count to ten. Don't lose sight of your blossoming bank balance and all the living space you've reclaimed. You have expanded your horizons, you now know more about computers and the Internet than you ever imagined. The parade hasn't passed you by. You're riding the Internet bandwagon!

PART III

Addiction: The Closet Mining Crossroads

CHAPTER 12

Your Well Has Run Dry: What Now?

> ➤ **A View from the Crossroads**
> ➤ **You Have What You Need—Do You Have What It Takes?**

All closet miners arrive at the same crossroads.
They eventually run out of stuff to sell.
Donald Trump should build a casino there.
It'd probably do very well.

Your house hasn't looked this good in years! You wouldn't part with another thing. But just as you were beginning to get the hang of it, you realize that you're running out of stuff to auction. The money you earned from your Internet auctions is burning a hole in your pocket. Every time you open your mailbox you're bummed out—no more checks to cash. You miss the action, the buzz; panic sets in.

You're going through Internet auction cold turkey! All closet miners experience similar withdrawal symptoms. In my heyday it never dawned on me that I'd run out of stuff to sell. I hit a wall around three dozen auctions. The bidding suddenly stopped. It appeared no one was really interested in my two unopened RCA Hi-8 video cassettes at any price—and even if they were, what would two video cassettes fetch?

There would be no more $50, $100, or $200 paydays. I spent my closet mining booty on a laser printer, an inkjet printer, a scanner, a USB hub, and a digital camera, all top of the line. I invested in digital photography to make my Internet auctions easier. Now I faced a conundrum. There was nothing left to photograph!

A View from the Crossroads

There's a fork in the road. Down one path, you walk away. It leads you back to where you were before Internet auctions. You retire a little wealthier and a little wiser.

Down the other, you stay in the game by reinventing yourself as a professional Internet auctioneer. This path leads to the inevitable question, *what am I going to sell?* If you aren't a professional retailer or wholesaler, answering this question is the first of many obstacles you'll encounter.

End of the Free Ride

Your Internet auction profits encompass more than the money you put in the bank; they include the square footage you reclaimed by uncluttering your environment. The value of real estate is based on square footage. If you have a nine hundred square foot apartment worth $100 thousand, and you freed up ninety square feet, you reclaimed $10 thousand worth of usable living space. The greatest thing about closet mining is that the inventory cost you zilch! You weren't using it. It was worthless—to you. What's the markup on a worthless belonging?

Unfortunately, the free ride is over now! The second hump ex-closet miners face, after they figure out what to sell, is that they now need to pay for inventory. You can't auction what you don't have; you must ante up some cash! Most manufacturers require a minimum purchase amounting to hundreds of dollars, plus shipping. Many businesses won't deal with you, even if you have the moolah, unless you have a resale number. You must apply to your state for a reseller's license before you can deal with these companies.

Finding Your Golden Goose

The only people I know who've gotten really rich off Internet auctions are the owners of eBay and its investors. Few sellers pull in the big bucks, although thousands earn respectable livings. Many others, like myself, use Internet auctions to supplement their primary income.

Beyond the closet mining crossroads Internet auctions are a business. The capital investment required to get a start-up off the ground pales in comparison to the amount of time and energy it consumes. The object of the Internet auction exercise is to locate dependable niche products that can generate multiple bids. This requires trial and error; you must test-market several products to see how they perform under real-world conditions. You'll spend endless hours creating new HTML ads, only to junk most of them. This process of elimination can be frustrating as well as time-consuming. Your self-esteem may suffer when an Internet auction you've invested energy and money in fails miserably!

A proven product that garners multiple bids is the Internet auction equivalent of shooting fish in a barrel. One good ad is all it takes for the profits to start rolling in. You can relist the auction time and again on multiple sites in multiple categories. A good niche product is the proverbial goose that lays the golden egg, a reward for all your trial and error. My golden goose turned out to be a Kit-Cat clock!

You Have What You Need—Do You Have What It Takes?

You have the tools and knowledge necessary to make it as a professional auctioneer, but do you have the skills and disposition? If your answer is yes, the following chapters will guide you. Every professional I know has a few aces hidden up his or her sleeve. I'll reveal mine and get others to reveal theirs.

On a scale of 1 to 10, I'm only a 4 or a 5 when it comes to being a professional auctioneer. I average a couple of dozen auctions a week. By contrast, there are professionals who run ten times that. I have one niche product, thus far, that has withstood the test of time and the ravages of rip-offs and competition. Several others have shown fleeting promise only to crash and burn.

Hot one month, cold the next, most Internet auctions have a limited shelf life. Successful auctions are knocked off with shocking regularity. The competition is vicious and the low-balling widespread. The very thing that makes Internet auctions so appealing to buyers—low prices—is what makes them so onerous for sellers. Many auctioneers sell products at cost simply to drive business to their Web site. I must admit I've used this tactic on occasion. More often than that I've been the victim of it, however.

Get Rich Quick?

You won't get rich from Internet auctions, but they can add thousands of dollars a year to your bank account. Would you like to work for yourself, call your own shots, be your own boss? You can be in business 24 hours a day, seven days a week, 365 days a year on the Internet, and run your entire empire in your underwear from the comfort of your own living room. Stop wearing makeup, grow a beard, stay up all night, sleep all day: Internet auctions offer freedom! As I'm fond of saying, you get out of them what you put into them.

CHAPTER 13

The Sheriff of eBay: Tales from the Not-So-OK Corral

As I stood at the Internet auction crossroads, delirium set in. I'm an artist: I'd rather reinvent the wheel than buy one from the Pep Boys! I wanted to offer the Internet auction public something never before available, an original creation. I was fixated on markup and profit. A perfect niche product would cost nothing, I reasoned; its profit would therefore be infinite.

My model was based on my first bid: Microsoft Office for $17. I never got over the fact that I paid eight bucks for information that cost the auctioneer nothing. He didn't even have to invest in a stamp. Upon receipt of payment the auctioneer e-mailed the winning bidders a password to a secure Web site from which they could download a list containing a handful of distributors liquidating Microsoft Office Pro. The Web site wasn't even a real Web site. It was the guy's AOL FTP space secured by a JavaScript password. What chutzpah, what audacity, what sheer brilliance!

Over the next few weeks I wondered and wandered and pondered what to sell. I prowled flea markets with my new digital camera searching for bargains that I could auction. I crawled the Internet, search engine by search engine, looking for wholesale products that would sustain a substantial markup. I wondered what I could invent that would take the Internet auction world by storm.

The Perfect Auction Item

It hit me like a bolt of lightning and snapped me out of my stupor! It was there in my head all along. It would cost me nothing and I could sell it for ten bucks; there was nothing remotely like it. It was a first, entirely original! "It" was a free Web site with a built-in shopping cart that even a novice could set up in minutes. I had created one—my first in a long line of Web sites—a month earlier.

iCAT, owned by Intel, was one of the first companies to jump on the e-commerce bandwagon. They offered a complete e-commerce package, soup to nuts, tailored to brick-and-mortar retailers with limited Internet experience. With innovative Web-based software, iCAT enabled a merchant to design and stock a virtual store in under an hour by filling out simple Web forms. Once created, the virtual store was placed in the iCAT Mall, the granddaddy of Internet shopping malls. iCAT was running a promotion to drum up business at the time. They were offering a free virtual store for life in the iCAT Mall! The only catch was you were limited to ten items. If you expanded beyond that, iCAT would start charging. Since I had zilch, ten items sounded like a lot.

I called iCAT to sound them out about having my customers take advantage of their promotion. They were most enthusiastic. I never got around to telling them that my customers would be winners of an Internet auction promoting their promotion. Without asking for any explanation they said they'd be happy to accommodate my customers. The free promotion was open to one and all!

I felt like I'd discovered the pot of gold at the end of the rainbow as I sat down to create an ad for the "free Web site" auction. My ad was geared to eBay sellers, not buyers, which is what I thought made it so unusual. I spent the better part of a day writing copy and creating artwork. I wanted it to be perfect! To characterize this work as ambitious would be a major understatement—it's the *War and Peace* of Internet auction ads! Figure 13.1 presents it in all its glory. Man, did it cause trouble!

It was early 1999. eBay was still young and I was in my own Internet auction infancy. I had not accumulated a feedback rating of 10 yet or I definitely would have listed the ad as a Featured Dutch auction. I had that much confidence in it—a sure sign of inexperience and hubris! Because of my sub-10 feedback rating I was relegated to listing each auction separately. To achieve the kind of results that a Dutch auction would, I decided to list a few dozen auctions in several different categories.

I gave up after 18 listings. I was using MS Internet Explorer, which was incompatible with eBay, and each listing became a grueling ordeal. After each error I pounded my desk and cursed out loud. My friend Paul, who was visiting from Bali, had the presence of mind to tear me away from my computer.

Things looked brighter the next day when I logged on to eBay. Four of my "free Web site" auctions generated bids overnight. I felt vindicated. All of my aggravation and hard work had not been for naught. The bids started piling up! Over the next few days I received several more. All the while I kept gloating to myself about how smart I was. I was getting ten dollars a bid for information that cost me zilch. I had eight or nine bids the night before my auctions were scheduled to close and had every reason to expect a few more. And this was just the first week!

Figure 13.1 *Although it went to absurd lengths, note the TLC poured into this ad's custom graphics and copy.*

> No special software is necessary besides your Web Browser. You will manage your website from the privacy of your own home or office computer, monitoring traffic and sales statistics while receiving up to the minute customer-feedback and online order status. In essence, you will be provided with all the information and technology you need to effectively manage your business, and to market your products and services. If you already have a website, your store can even provide links to it.
>
> ## INVALUABLE TOOLS
>
> All this and a whole lot more is at your disposal absolutely free of charge!
>
> - **SALES REPORTS** - Information about your orders and customers over a specified period of time.
> - **CUSTOMER REPORTS** - You can generate customer lists and detailed order summaries at any time.
> - **TRAFFIC AND HIT REPORTS** - You will receive real-time statistics on which items and sections in your store are being viewed.
>
> ## IT TOOK MORE TIME TO CREATE THIS PAGE THAN TO CREATE MY STORE
>
> That's how simple it is. I'll even go one better. It's actually fun! The whole process is geared toward simplicity.
>
> ## WHAT'S THE CATCH?
>
> As you can imagine, this kind of technology doesn't grow on trees. Many of your favorite websites are powered by it and they pay tens of thousands of dollars for the privilege. So, what makes you so lucky that you qualify for free?
>
> This offer is being tendered by a company which already has the high-end market sewn-up. To continue growing they must expand their market-share. To accomplish that they have placed a bet on the small time entrepreneur, mom-and-pop operators like you and me. They believe in us. They believe they will profit in the long-term by providing this extraordinary opportunity now, because they believe we will succeed and become their next generation of paying customers!
>
> ## HERE'S THE DEAL
>
> Your store will remain free as long as your inventory is held to ten products or less at any given moment! You can replace existing items with new items as often as you like, but as soon as your inventory expands to eleven (11) items or beyond, a monthly fee will commence. The rational is you will be compelled to expand your store beyond ten products once you see how successful it is. They're betting on your success!
>
> The cost of expansion is extremely reasonable, fifty bucks a month for fifty products. By the time you blossom into a Mega-Site with 3000 items, your inventory will cost less than 11 cents per product.
>
> ## MONEY-BACK GUARANTEE
>
> I am not affiliated with this company in any way, nor can I predict how long this offer will be valid. If you want to qualify for this golden opportunity, act now, before it's too late! This information is guaranteed for 30 days of the postmark on the envelope in which it is received. If for any reason you are unable to obtain your free website within those 30 days, simply return the envelope for a full refund.
>
> **PAYMENT** By Money Orders, Cashiers Checks, & Personal Checks
> **SHIPPING** Please Remember To Include An Additional **$2.00** For Shipping & Handling
> **HANDLING** Orders Will Be Shipped Promptly.

Figure 13.1 *Continued*

Welcome, You've Got Mail

My heart sank the moment I logged on to AOL. As I look back on this e-mail from eBay, I can still feel my horror and anguish.

> *Subj: NOTICE: eBay Registration Suspension—Site Interference*
>
> *Date: 3/7/1999 6:11:16 AM Pacific Standard Time*
>
> *From: XXXXXXX@ebay.com*
>
> *To: zenweb0@aol.com*
>
> *Dear zenweb,*
>
> *We regret to inform you that your eBay account has been suspended for the following reason:*
>
> ** Using Any Mechanism To Interfere with eBay's Site and/or Operations*
>
> *While this suspension is active, you are prohibited from registering under a new account name or using our system in any way. Any attempt to reregister will result in permanent account suspension with no possibility of reinstatement. This suspension does not relieve you of your agreed-upon obligation to pay any fees you may owe to eBay. All responses or appeals regarding this suspension must be made directly to the Customer Support representative indicated in the signature of this notice, or you can write to eBay at the following address:*
>
> *Regards,*
>
> *XXXXXXX(XXXXXXX@ebay.com)*
>
> *eBay Inc*

Using Any Mechanism To Interfere with eBay's Site and/or Operations? eBay was impugning me for misdeeds I wasn't even capable of perpetrating! Their accusation made me sound like a master hacker hell-bent on sabotage. It had to be a mistake! To cancel my auctions without warning and suspend my membership without explanation was a drastic overreaction on eBay's part; it was totally incomprehensible. I took a deep breath, counted to ten, and responded to XXXXXXX@ebay.com by e-mail.

> *Subj: Re: NOTICE: eBay Registration Suspension—Site Interference*
>
> *Date: 3/8/1999*
>
> *To: XXXXXXX@ebay.com*

In a message dated 3/7/1999 6:11:16 AM Pacific Standard Time, XXXXXXX@ebay.com writes:

<< *Dear zenweb (zenweb0@aol.com),*

We regret to inform you that your eBay account has been suspended for the following reason:

* Using Any Mechanism To Interfere with eBay's Site and/or Operations >>

XXXXXXX,

This is a giant mistake. I did nothing to Interfere with eBay's Site and/or Operations, whatsoever. Nor would I even know how to. What exactly do you think I did? I spent over two hours manually re-listing my bids Saturday and even had to contact your tech support department because eBay's software was giving so many error messages. After all that effort eBay wants to suspend me? What exactly am I being accused of? I believe eBay owes me an apology, instant reinstatement, and each of my auctions started over from scratch. I would appreciate a prompt reply.

Michael Weber

The same customer service representative responded and the following exchange ensued:

<< *Hello,*

Your account was suspended for intentionally mass-listing, in random, unrelated categories, your information item. This is considered deliberate site interference, and cannot be tolerated on eBay. Thank you.

Regards,

—SafeHarbor Investigations Team >>

XXXXXXX ,

I'm sure you understand I did this <u>unintentionally</u>. I don't feel I should be unjustly punished for a minor misunderstanding. Am I now free to place new auctions on eBay? Since I didn't place the offending info randomly, but in the computer and software categories—where it would appear they belong—where do you suggest I place it? Finally, will my account be credited for the 18 pulled auctions?

Thank you,

M Weber

I felt my articulate and sincere response would clear up any misunderstanding. Instead, I got back this smarmy form letter telling me to go jump in the lake.

Subj: *Receipt of your message*

***** PLEASE DO NOT REPLY TO THIS MESSAGE AS YOU WILL NOT RECEIVE A RESPONSE FROM THIS MAILBOX******

Thank you for writing to eBay Customer Support! Your query is *very* important to us.

Please note the following information; you might find the answer to your question here! If your auction was ended for one of the reasons below, please consider this your response so that we may dedicate our resources to helping users that require specific assistance. If your question is not answered here, please contact moreinfo@ebay.com for further help.

We have several reasons for the ending of auctions, ALL OF WHICH ARE NOT DISPUTABLE. They are as follows:

1. ADVERTISEMENT: Your item must be listed as an actual auction and not as an advertisement for your item or service. We allow goods or services being offered to advertise a business, however, eBay does not allow auction listings to be used as advertisements for soliciting potential customers for an item or service by offering it for direct purchase (that is, bypassing the auction format).

2. BESTIALITY: These items are illegal to sell.

3. BONUSES, GIVEAWAYS, PRIZES: eBay does not allow the listing of auctions that contain bonus items, giveaways, or random drawings or prizes as an enticement for bidders as such promotions are illegal lotteries in many states.

4. BOOTLEGS, PIRATED MEDIA, ETC.: eBay does not allow the listing of "pirated", "bootlegged", counterfeit or otherwise unauthorized uses of copyright or trademarked audio, video, or other media. eBay works with copyright and intellectual property owners to protect such rights. For more information on piracy, please go to the following page: http://pages.ebay.com/aw/faq-piracy.html

5. BUDDY PROGRAM: Items reported as infringing upon the trademark/copyrights of a particular company/individual. You will have to contact the manufacturer in question as eBay does not make these determinations. For more information on the Buddy Program, please go to the following page:

http://pages.ebay.com/aw/buddy-program.html

6. BULK EMAIL: eBay does not allow the listing of auctions for lists of bulk email addresses.

7. COUNTERFEIT/REPLICA ITEMS: Per the terms of our New User Agreement,"...6.2 Your Information and the sale of your item(s) on eBay: (a) shall not infringe any third party's copyright, patent, trademark, trade secret or other proprietary rights or rights of publicity or privacy;..." You should contact the manufacturer in question with questions.

8. CROSS POSTING SERVICE AND INFORMATIONAL ITEMS: Items that offer a service or information pertaining to a service, may only be listed in the Miscellaneous : Services : Information Services category.

9. DO NOT BID—SINGLE ITEM: eBay does not allow "do not bid" notices to be listed as auction listings.

10. DUTCH AUCTION CHOICE: The offering of multiple items in a Dutch Auction that are not identical is not permitted at this time. ALL items must be identical.

11. FEATURED AUCTIONS: Please go to the following URL for a list of items that are not acceptable for a Featured Auction Listing: http://cgi.ebay.com/aw-cgi/eBayISAPI.dll?Featured

12. FIREWORKS, EXPLOSIVES: eBay does not allow the listing of fireworks, explosives, or other incendiary devices because they are illegal to sell.

13. HIGH SHIPPING CHARGES: eBay does not allow the listing of Dutch Auction items that start at less than $1 but state a shipping and handling charge of more than $5 in an attempt to circumvent eBay auction fees. You may relist the item but only with either a starting price of $1 or more, or with total shipping and handling charges of not more than $5.

14. ILLEGAL ITEMS: Self-explanatory.

15. ITEM EMAILED BEFORE AUCTION ENDS: eBay does not allow the listing of items which invite the bidder to receive the product via email before the auction is completed. You may relist the item if you choose but only minus any such offer.

16. *ITEM FOR DIRECT SALE: eBay does not allow the listing of items that instruct bidders to not bid and/or offer the item for direct purchase from the seller since this effectively circumvents eBay auction fees.*

17. *LINKS TO OTHER AUCTION SERVICES: eBay does not allow the listing of auctions which include links (static or live) to other online auction services.*

18. *LIVE ANIMALS: eBay does not allow the listing of live animals for bid.*

19. *MULTI-LEVEL MARKETING: eBay does not allow the listing of Multi-Level Marketing (MLM) programs as auction items.*

20. *MULTI-LISTING: Multiple listings of similar items must use a Dutch Action format and be listed in a single appropriate category.*

21. *PER BID ADDITIONAL PURCHASE: eBay does not allow the listing of items which contain an offer to purchase additional items per the bid price, since this effectively circumvents eBay auction fees.*

22. *RAFFLES, LOTTERIES: eBay does not allow the listing of raffles or lotteries as auction items, since they are illegal in many states.*

23. *RISQUE TITLES FOR FEATURED AUCTIONS: eBay does not allow sellers of Featured Auctions to list titles for their auctions that are risqué or sexually provocative.*

24. *SELLER SETS RESERVE: Sellers are obliged to sell their non-Reserve Price Auction item at the current high bid to the current high bidder shown at the time of the auction's close regardless of any statement to the contrary that a seller may include within the item's description.*

25. *SIGNPOST: Your auction must be listed as an actual auction as opposed to a "sign post" notice pointing to another auction item.*

26. *USED UNDERGARMENTS: We do not allow used, unwashed undergarments for bid at eBay.*

eBay Customer Support—We care!

---

eBay Inc.

Your Personal Trading Community (tm)

"Please do not reply to this message as you will not receive a response from this mailbox"? I saw red. I had visions of a handful of pimply college kids in a garage somewhere in San Jose pulling the strings of a heartless corporation. But my battle with eBay would have to be fought another day. I was scheduled to leave town. If the mix-up wasn't resolved by the time I returned, I'd have no option but to go on the warpath.

I'm not a litigious person by nature. The only lawsuit I've ever been party to was a class action suit against Compaq Computer alleging some monkey business that caused their stock to plummet. A top New York law firm contacted me. Over the course of time I became acquainted with their lead attorney.

I returned to town three weeks after eBay gave me the boot and logged on to their site. My membership was still suspended. I'd had enough! I called the lead attorney from the class action law firm and explained my dilemma. He advised me to send a certified letter to eBay's CEO notifying them of their blunder and demanding immediate reinstatement of my membership. If eBay failed to respond within two weeks, the attorney asked me to get back in touch. I fired off the following letter, a warning shot across eBay's bow:

Ms.(eBay's Chief Executive Officer),

I know you're busy so I'll get right to the point. eBay's treatment of me has been unconscionable. I have been treated like a petty criminal and my registration has been blocked for two months for the ominous sounding offense of *intentionally interfering with eBay's system resources* by posting auctions in random categories. Repeated requests for an explanation of what I am being accused of have been met with the silent treatment. So, for the record:

A) If I did anything to interfere with eBay's resources, I apologize. It was definitely unintentional.

B) There was nothing random whatsoever about the categories in which I posted the auctions in question.

C) I am not a master hacker and would not know how to interfere with eBay's system resources even if I wanted to.

I am writing to you on the advice of my attorney. I want my account reactivated immediately. If it is not activated by May 17,

1999, I will consider legal action. I find it surprising that a company with eBay's potential would treat customers in such an unjust and discriminatory manner.

Sincerely,

Michael Weber

CC: Pierre Omidyar

The Sheriff of eBay Rides to the Rescue

Don't let the khakis or his youthful appearance fool you. Rob Chesnut is a man to be reckoned with! Before joining eBay as associate General counsel, Chesnut spent a decade in Washington D.C. prosecuting racketeering and corruption cases for the federal government. He traded in his suspenders in 1999 and pinned on a badge for eBay.

Even if 99.98 percent of eBay's transactions close without a hitch, as eBay claims, .02 percent of several million transactions a month adds up to a lot of unhappy customers, a lot of complaints, a lot of scams, and a lot of rip-offs! eBay hired Chesnut to apply the same sensibility to Internet con artists that he did to mobsters and racketeers.

I was one of the 0.02 percent with a legitimate gripe. My letter to eBay's CEO wound up on Rob's desk and he called me. I was relieved that eBay responded. Rob was credible; he gave me his background and admitted that eBay might have acted rashly. He apologized for eBay's handling of the matter and reassured me that they were training and expanding their staff to resolve these kinds of issues more efficiently. He was going to conduct an investigation, like any good sheriff would, and get back to me.

Rob got back to me in less than 24 hours. He had concluded that my complaint was justified. I had been swept up in a dragnet designed to stop denial-of-service attacks, the very same kind of attack which brought eBay, Yahoo, and e-Trade to their collective knees a year later. My automatic suspension was triggered by the 18 Free Web Site submissions. eBay only allows seven duplicate listings, so technically I was also at fault. Rob conceded that the penalty eBay dealt me for such a minor infraction was inappropriate, and he apologized again for his company's behavior. He'd already reinstated my membership and credited my account with $50 for my trouble. Rob asked if there was anything further he could do? I answered yes and asked him if I could interview him.

An Interview with the Sheriff of eBay

Michael Weber interviewed Rob Chesnut, the Sheriff of eBay, on July 21, 2000. Kevin Pursglove of eBay's PR team was also present.

MW: Rob, in my book I describe you as having swapped your suspenders at the Department of Justice for a badge and a pair of khakis at eBay. How would you describe your function?

Rob: I don't wear a suit and tie anymore, like I used to every day. I've got my khakis and polo shirt now. I work on a number of issues, probably the most interesting of which is what should be sold on eBay, and dealing with items that are problems that might be illegal or otherwise improper, and trying to come up with sort of the boundaries and rules that people live by while they're on eBay.

MW: Your official title is what, Corporate Counsel?

Rob: Associate General Counsel.

MW: Associate General Counsel. But you specialize more in the troubleshooting arena?

Rob: I think that's fair. I receive litigation; I work on government relations. I have a number of different functions. But certainly troubleshooting and the area of problems with types of items being listed is a significant part of my job.

MW: I just read an article about two burglars from New England who sold some stolen booty on eBay. For my readers' sakes, what should bidders look out for when they come across an item that looks like a steal?

Rob: Looks like a steal? Well, it might be a steal, because there are some great deals out there. But on the other hand, you also need to realize a fundamental lesson that everybody probably learned from their parents, and that is: Sometimes, if something looks like it's too good to be true, it probably is. So buyers ought to use good judgment and recognize that, and investigate things for themselves...look into it and ask questions.

MW: Do due diligence?

Rob: Yes. Absolutely.

MW: You know the name of my book is *Confessions of an Internet Auction Junkie*: Are there actual Internet auction junkies? How serious would you say addiction is, because my title is sort of tongue-in-cheek.

Rob: It's not in the DSM yet. I don't think it's recognized, and no psychiatrists are specializing in it. But I talk to people all the time who look at me and say, "I'm upset with you. Look what you've done to me." Or, "Look what you've done to my wife or my kids or my husband," they spend an hour a day on eBay. But they have a smile when they say it, so they just love it.

MW: It's now July 2000, and I was recently flamed by somebody who berated me for auctioning a 1999 model Kit-Cat under Vintage Clocks. Is flaming prevalent on eBay, and what's your advice when it comes to e-mail and *Netiquette* in general?

Rob: Well one thing when it comes to e-mail is that people seem to feel more uninhibited when they send e-mails. There's a lot more emotion and they tend to say things they wouldn't say in a phone call or face-to-face. I think people are much more accusatory and nasty in e-mail because it's so anonymous.

MW: So, what's your advice? We already have road rage. Are e-mail rage and Internet rage inevitable byproducts?

Rob: I do think people ought to think about what they send to someone else in e-mail. When they're writing it, they should think, "Is this something I'd say to a person face-to-face?", and recognize that e-mail can be a benefit, but some things you say can also be misinterpreted. Sometimes I think people should be a little more careful about what they say in e-mail. Because I have seen situations where things can escalate and people can get in nasty e-mail battles with each other, where if they had just spoken to each other on the phone, they'd probably have been friends in five minutes.

MW: My biggest foible as an Internet auctioneer is that I hate to leave negative feedback. Am I not doing my part?

Rob: Yeah. Well, the opposite also applies. Some people leave negative feedback too quickly. You know, they'll send a personal check for an item, and if they haven't gotten it in 10 days.... And they don't think about calling the person and trying to work it out first. We now have a professional mediation service called Square Trade that I highly recommend. A lot of times all you need is a neutral third party who can take a difficult situation and bring people together. I would encourage people to make every effort to resolve something before leaving negative feedback. The other side is that some people take feedback too seriously.

MW: Too seriously? How?

Rob: There are people who literally fall apart.

MW: That's amazing. I have a feedback rating of about 250 positives and zero negatives and I consider it pure luck!

Rob: Yeah, it is. Because in real life….

MW: Because I've screwed up enough to deserve one or two negatives!

Rob: If you deal with a hundred people, you're going to have a problem sometime. It may have nothing to do with you—it's just because people don't always get along. And people, I think, get really upset when they get a negative, and what they should realize, if you deal with a hundred people and 99 love you, you're doing great! But I think sometimes people get really worked up about a negative. I would encourage people to try to be more cautious before leaving a negative and try to work things out using mediation, or maybe even picking up the phone. But I'd also encourage people not to get too worked up when they get a negative, because in life, if we all got 99s or 98s…we'd be really happy!

MW: Do deadbeats qualify for leaving negative feedback?

Rob: Sometimes… you can deal with it by filing a credit form with eBay, which will generate a negative e-mail to the nonpaying bidder.

Kevin: Mike, can I add something here?

MW: Sure, Kevin.

Kevin: If you had a bad experience with somebody, wouldn't you have wanted to know that others had bad experiences with that individual too?

MW: Yes, I would. I feel remiss about this, which is why I brought it up. In the book, I advise readers to leave negative feedback. Does eBay have a policy toward chronic deadbeats and bid retractors?

Rob: Well, bid retractors…you should have a good reason for doing it. And what we do is, your bid retractions are now available, so other users can see how many times you've retracted your bid. And therefore sellers may decide to cancel your bid, because they don't want to deal with you. Which is up to the seller; that's fine. So, if you are retracting bids frequently, I think it will only hurt your ability to do business in the community.

MW: Is there a magic number? I mean if a member gets like 6 deadbeat complaints or has 10 bid retractions?

Rob: You'll get a warning the first time you're a deadbeat. And the second time you'll probably get a short time suspension, and the third time would be a lifetime one. But even that is flexible, because it may depend on the number of transactions you do. If your feedback is zero, and you get two "non-pay bidders," you'll get suspended. If your feedback is 100 you'll get more leniency.

MW: So there is a formula?

Rob: The formula, in many cases, is good judgment.

MW: Good judgment. Well, thank you for that, Rob! That's how we met. You were very up-front and humane with me when you realized that I was erroneously targeted by some software glitch.

Rob: Well, we make mistakes too, but we do our best. We get a lot of e-mail. When you're dealing with hundreds of thousands of transactions per day, you're going to make some mistakes.

MW: We all do. What's important is that you recognize and learn from them. Do you have any parting words for my readers?

Rob: Nothing deep. Use good judgment, be smart, and have fun!

CHAPTER 14

Microsoft Office for $17: Secrets and Guides

> The Wholesaler's Guide Saga
> Selling Information Online
> The Secret behind Guides
> Buy It—Sell It—Pass It on
> Who Says There's No Free Lunch?

More people have bid on and purchased Microsoft Office Pro 97 than just about any other product in Internet auction history. In early 1999, hundreds of Internet auctioneers earned a living selling just this one product. They purchased minimum amounts of the OEM version from liquidators at $15 to $17 a copy and auctioned them off at $20 to $30. There's no way to calculate the number of copies sold, but hundreds of thousands would be a conservative estimate.

Microsoft itself was at the root of this fire sale. Office 2000 was just around the corner and the company didn't want to get stuck with millions of copies of an outdated product. Microsoft didn't factor Internet auctions into the equation, however. How could it? In 1999 Internet auctions were an unknown quantity, a relatively new phenomenon.

The Wholesaler's Guide Saga

The following story is true but the names have been changed to protect the innocent:

Like the magician who reveals a trick, Rodney was a man with a plan. Instead of auctioning Microsoft Office Pro for $25 like hundreds of other sellers, he auctioned a list of distributors who were liquidating it for $17 or less.

It was a brilliant idea that garnered hundreds of bids, including my first. I couldn't pass up such a good secret even though I had no intention of selling the product. My second bid was for Microsoft Office Pro, of course. It cost me $23, $327 below the manufacturer's suggested list price.

When Microsoft discovered what was happening it leaned on the auction sites to lean on their customers and OEM software auctions were banned. Because so many people have bought and sold Microsoft Office Pro, this product, like Beanie Babies, will always be an integral chapter of Internet auction's history.

Rodney retired his "Where to buy Microsoft Office for $17" auction when the heat came down, and he posted a red flag on his Web site advising his customers not to auction it. He looks back on it now as ancient history.

When I first contacted him and brought the subject up, Rodney was quick to point out that the "Wholesaler's Guide" was just a small part of his eBay sales, and not his most creative or successful project. He added, "I have several of my own software programs for sale on eBay which have been much more successful: a bid reminder program, an ad generator, a resource guide package, and more recently a database program for eBay sellers. Like the 'Wholesaler's Guide,' they are inexpensive to produce (after the initial outlay of development time), but they are much more a part of my profile at eBay."

Rodney is truly an Internet auction pioneer. He joined eBay in its infancy, on May 18, 1997. His About Me page was featured in the first eBay newsletter—and when the company conducted a recent usability study in San Jose, eBay invited Rodney to participate. Rodney was in the vanguard of developing and selling software utilities customized for the Internet auction marketplace. His latest offering, released in December 1999, is the Seller's Database, a tool for tracking auction sales. The Seller's Database stores customer records (like spreadsheets) and reminds you when to ship, leave feedback, send late-pay reminders, and request credits. Today, Rodney has 109 items listed for auction on eBay and his feedback rating is a whopping 2,678.

Rodney is a model netizen who prides himself on having given something back to the Internet auction community. His reluctance to discuss the "Where to Buy Microsoft Office for $17" auction was therefore understandable. "The 'MS Office Wholesaler's Guide' was information I bought on eBay and only distributed for a very short while," Rodney points out. His anxieties were allayed when I informed him my curiosity was generic. My interest in that auction was about its formula, not its substance.

Selling Information Online

Guides contain valuable information people will pay for. They're often marketed as *secrets*. Selling information is quite profitable because it costs little or nothing to obtain. It resides in a file on your hard drive and can be sold over and over again. Some secrets and guides are original creations like my "Free Web site" auction. Others, like the "MS Office Wholesaler's Guide," are purchased for a small sum, or knocked off and repackaged as exclusive and original. This isn't to suggest the information they contain is any less useful. Successful secrets and guides generally contain useful information.

Several people who bid on my "Free Web site" auction knocked it off. Some got creative and totally repackaged it. Others were brazen enough to steal the whole kit-and-caboodle—copy, artwork, and headline—and run it as is. There was nothing I could do about that. The auction ran its course after receiving about 50 bids and I was on the lookout for a new information product. That's when I discovered Megadisk.

The Secret behind Guides

Megadisk really opened my eyes! A CD-ROM that purportedly contained a treasure trove of entrepreneurial secrets and tricks, Megadisk auctioned for only $8.99. But that wasn't its hook. Megadisk's main selling point was resale rights. Bidding on it entitled the buyers to resell Megadisk, or any part of it, as often as they liked.

The information contained on the CD-ROM ranged from excellent to unusable. It was a hodge-podge of compilations. How to be a private eye, how to be an Internet spy, the Beanie Baby trader's guide, the eBay seller's guide, the wholesaler's liquidator and drop-shippers guide, auction ad templates, JPGs and animated GIFs, and links to free software information and services were just a few of the bases it touched.

I thought I knew something about Internet auctions. Suddenly I felt very naive! These very same auctions had been staring me in the face for months. No wonder Megadisk was selling so well. Half the people selling how-to guides on the Internet appeared to be getting their information from this CD-ROM.

Buy It—Sell It—Pass It on

Here I was burning my brains out to come up with an original idea when the answer was right in front of me. Megadisk contained a small gem called "Business Pack." It was a grand compilation built around two large HTML documents. The information on it was fresh and useful. The auctioneer had compiled it recently and apparently poured his heart into it. I would have done several things differently, so that's exactly what I did! I added a few touches and twists, gave it a new look, and christened it "Profit-Master" (see Figure 14.1).

Profit-Master sold like gangbusters for a while at $10 a bid. After investing in labels and floppy disks, Profit-Master cost 67 cents per copy to ship, including envelopes and stamps. The auction site charged another sixty-five cents. The remaining $8.68—658 percent—was pure profit. I told you selling information is profitable!

I stopped auctioning Profit-Master some time ago and went on to bigger and better things. I don't feel guilty about having sold it then or now; the information it contained was extremely useful. I still use it often. I also feel that I added to the original both aesthetically and in content by making it easier to navigate. In the final analysis, reselling information purchased from others is as old as time immemorial and a stage all Internet auctioneers seem to go through on the road to finding successful niche products to call their own.

Spawn of Megadisk

Like some mutating virus, a majority of the information products auctioned on the Internet today are derived from or duplicates of Megadisk. This morning I did a keyword search on auctions containing the text "Beanie +wholesale" and discovered 167 listings on eBay alone. They ranged in price from $3.99 to $14.99. After perusing several dozen auctions I didn't find one that wasn't based on Megadisk. Whether you want to buy it or avoid it the keywords are the same: Beanie, Spy, Private Eye, Wholesale, eBay, Make $XXXX, and Free.

Who Says There's No Free Lunch?

As a reward for having come this far I invite you to download Profit-Master from the *Confessions* CD-ROM. It's an extremely valuable resource for anyone involved in Internet marketing. My offer includes the resale rights! If you're so inclined, feel free to experiment with Profit-Master. Adopt and adapt it, rename it, and auction it as your own. Three or four winners will more than pay for this book! And you'll learn something in the process.

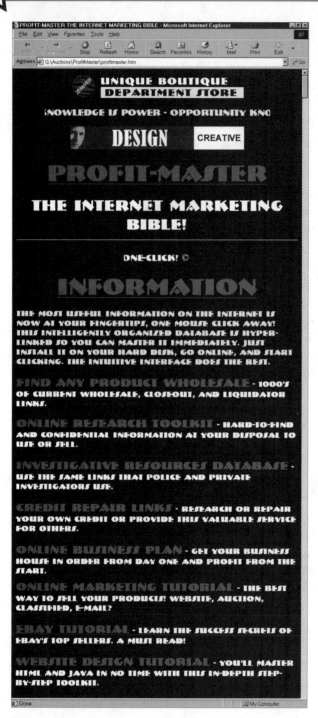

Figure 14.1 *That's me—the Man from Profit-Master.*

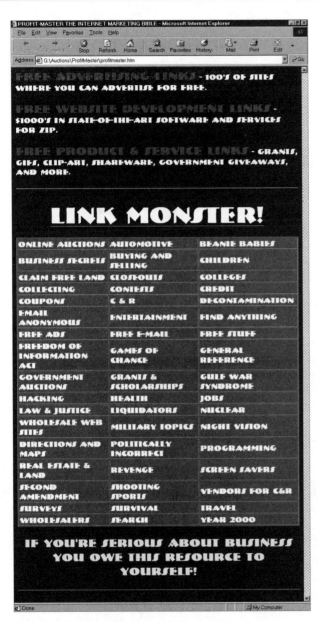

Figure 14.1 *Continued*

CHAPTER 15

Getting the Drop-Ship on Your Competition

> ➤ The Long and Winding Road
> ➤ The Drop-Shipping Advantage

I was on a long and winding road leading to a house atop a hill overlooking Laguna Beach, on my way to meet Arthur and Eileen Hirsch, manufacturers and distributors of the Kit-Cat clock. I wanted to make a good impression on them. A month before, we had struck a deal that at last made it possible for me to eke out a living as an Internet auctioneer. As my car approached their home at the top of the canyon I thought to myself, they must be doing well!

Arthur and Eileen are more than husband and wife. They are partners in business and partners in life. Eileen welcomed me warmly to the sprawling house from which they ran their little empire. At one end was a garage filled to the rafters with Kit-Cat clocks of every description. This was their shipping department, the clocks already spoken for by customers. "The warehouse and factory are 20 miles down the road in Torrance," Eileen told me.

At the other end of the house Arthur was on the phone in the den that served as the company's communications center. He came from Brooklyn and so did I. Arthur was also my father's name. We hit it off the minute he hung up the phone.

The Long and Winding Road

My route here was so circuitous it could properly be described as a fluke! The free Web site and Profit-Master auctions had run their course and I was looking for a new niche product to replace them.

Those auctions taught me a few lessons that now factored heavily in my search; the most apparent was that shipping is the biggest closet mining grind. No more laborious packaging and long lines at the post office for me—selling information was as easy as stuffing a floppy disk into an envelope and popping it in the corner mail box. I concluded that I was interested in auctioning products that could be shipped directly from the manufacturer to my customers in the future. This is known in the trade as drop-shipping.

In my quest for products that met this criterion I concentrated on the tried and true. One of my most fruitful closet mining auctions was for a Dunhill Roll-A-Gas butane lighter—which fetched over a hundred dollars as a result of the ad in Figure 15.1.

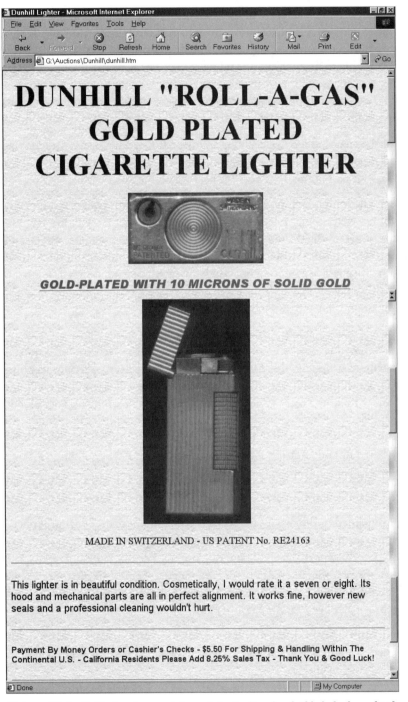

Figure 15.1 *Gold plated, patented, made in Switzerland: this baby brought the bidders out of the woodwork.*

In my travels I came across a lighter based on the Dunhill design called the Marquis. I contacted its distributors, who turned out to be Arthur and Eileen Hirsch, and that's what brought me on this pilgrimage. Arthur and Eileen were amenable to drop-shipping and we struck a deal on the phone. In addition to the Marquis, they carried several other lighters plus a full line of clocks. They invited me to auction everything they had, and suddenly I had a supplier and a distributor all rolled into one!

One of the clocks, the Kit-Cat, hung in my bedroom when I was little. It was a good omen! I auctioned several Marquis lighters the first week—and 16 Kit-Cat clocks. Figures 15.2 and 15.3 showcase the ads I used.

I'd been auctioning Arthur and Eileen's merchandise for over a month now and things were going splendidly. The best part was that I didn't have to touch a single product! I ran the auctions, processed the purchase orders, and pocketed the profits. Arthur and Eileen shipped the products and made their markup. Business was good. So good, in fact, that we decided to meet. Laguna Beach is short hop from L.A., and now here I was sipping Diet Pepsi with them on their sun-drenched patio.

Arthur and Eileen are an attractive and articulate couple who work side by side. "We got married after six years of dating and moved into a beautiful apartment overlooking the Hudson River." Said Eileen. "Arthur went to work for Cushman and Wakefield, a commercial real estate firm in New York City, and I took up tennis. Our lives changed in 1980 while visiting friends in La Jolla. We'd been considering relocation for a while. On a fluke, we drove our rental car through Laguna Canyon and were blown away by its beauty! Arthur and I started looking for a house that day. We found this one a few weeks later and we've been living here ever since!"

"Is that when you got involved with the Kit-Cat clock?" I inquired.

"No; I remained in the real estate rat race several more years," Arthur replied. "I worked from six in the morning 'til eight at night, schlepping from Century City to Newport Beach. Then, one night Eileen asked me a question I couldn't answer. She asked, 'Why did we move to California, Arthur? What good is this lifestyle if we can't take advantage of it as a family?' I realized at that moment I'd been sacrificing my family's quality of life for my career."

"Arthur turned his back on millions of dollars a year," Eileen said proudly. "He shed his suit for a pair of jeans and we started from scratch in the import-export business."

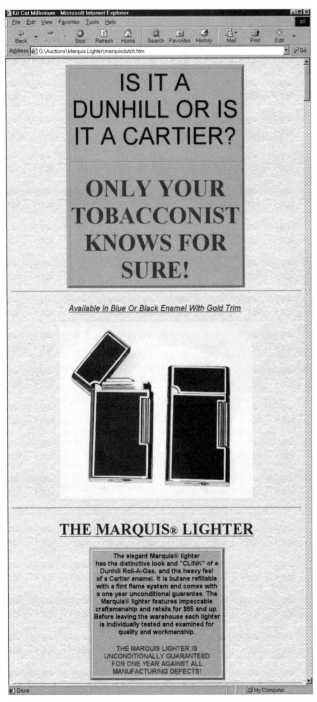

Figure 15.2 *I paraphrased a headline from an old Clairol ad most people are too young to remember.*

Figure 15.3 *The first Kit-Cat campaign. Note the similarity in layout to the Marquis lighter ad in Figure 15.2.*

"We invested in the California Clock Company, manufacturer of the Kit-Cat clock, in 1991," Arthur continued. "I needed all the help I could get and Eileen started pitching in. We've been a team ever since! The Kit-Cat clock had been around over 50 years and unfortunately the sales were waning. But there was something special about it. I remembered it from when I was a kid. It evoked fun and nostalgia and put a smile on the face of everybody who saw one. I wanted to bring the product back to life. I wanted to put a Kit-Cat clock in every store in America!"

"We haven't done that quite yet," Eileen chuckled. "But nowadays we sell over a million dollars a year in Kit-Cat clocks alone! So, what can we do for you, Michael?"

I felt so far in over my head that I couldn't even fake it. My background was in entertainment and advertising, not merchandising. I hadn't known a P.O. form from a P.O. box until Arthur showed me how to fill one out. Admitting that you know nothing is empowering, however. It enables you to ask questions with impunity. The Hirsches claim they found my naïveté refreshing. Like good mentors, they answered every question I hurled at them.

The Winning Formula

In a way this meeting was anticlimactic—we were already a success! We earned thousands of dollars together the first month, just cruising on autopilot. I bet everything on featured Dutch auctions in multiple categories for cigarette lighters, cigar humidors, and Kit-Cat clocks. Several models sold across the line but the Kit-Cat clocks were a bonanza, a bona fide hit! Don't forget, eBay was devised to satiate the needs of a Pez collector. The Kit-Cat orders piled up. People bid on two, three, five at a time! Arthur and Eileen shipped almost a hundred that first month. Neither the Hirsches nor I expected we'd be this successful. We laughed about our good fortune.

"Should I tell him?" Arthur beamed at Eileen.

"Tell me what?" I asked, feeling outside an inside joke. The truth was about to rear its ugly head! The Hirsches confessed that they went along with me at first because they felt they had nothing to lose. They weren't in the habit of drop-shipping goods for customers, or of offering credit to strangers, especially strangers who were admitted amateurs. The fact that this came up didn't surprise me in the least. I was thinking about it myself on the drive here. Arthur and Eileen could cut me out and run auctions of their own if they wished. I wanted to know one way or another before getting my hopes too high or investing too much time.

The fact of the matter is that the subject did come up; early on, Eileen suggested to Arthur that they could run their own Internet auctions. Arthur countered that auctions were tedious work requiring a sizable investment in time and money. Eileen didn't understand why Arthur, renown for driving a hard bargain, was giving me such a good deal. Arthur liked my pitch and I caught him on a slow day, he explained. Internet auctions were a new phenomenon and a base they didn't have covered. At the end of the day they mutually agreed that they had no inclination to become directly involved with what turned out to be a very lucrative market. They needed repeat customers like me for their business to thrive, and I was pulling my own load and deserved to reap my just reward. We made a dynamite team!

I welcomed their candor because I had a secret, too. I didn't intend to bring it up, but Arthur and Eileen made me feel so comfortable that I didn't hesitate. "Did you know that I'm writing a book about Internet auctions?" I asked. Arthur and Eileen looked a little surprised—perhaps they didn't believe me. After all, everybody in L.A. is supposedly writing a book or a screenplay.

"Actually, I'm writing a book proposal," I explained to Arthur and Eileen. "I'm not writing the book yet." They seemed genuinely interested.

"What's that?"

"A 40- or 50-page synopsis that agents submit to publishers," I answered. I think they believed me. They laughed out loud when I told them the title, *Confessions of an Internet Auction Junkie.*

Hanging out with Arthur and Eileen—and letting our hair down—put our deal on solid footing and cultivated a genuine friendship. If there's a lesson to be learned in all of this it's *follow your flukes!* I came in search of a cigarette lighter and found a Kit-Cat clock. You never know what's around the next bend, so follow your instincts.

The Drop-Shipping Advantage

Let's examine this deal in reverse. I didn't know diddly about business, but I knew I didn't want to ship anything. I didn't want to have to touch products, stock inventory, or pay for inventory in advance ever again. These were high goals, indeed, perhaps even unrealistic. But I didn't know any better. On the other hand, Arthur and Eileen shipped products for a living. They owned a warehouse full of Kit-Cat clocks and cigarette lighters that were in stock all the time, whether paid for or not. Our deal was made in heaven.

More manufacturers may be open to drop-shipping than you might imagine. They need to move merchandise in the same way you need qualified products to auction. Finding a manufacturer who'll drop-ship isn't the biggest hurdle—finding a great niche product is. You'll have to search long and hard to find a product as rewarding as the Kit-Cat clock has been for me. That's why I've written about it ad nauseam—for me Kit-Cat clocks have been like a slot machine stuck on triple 7!

I am often called the Kit-Cat King but I'm merely a loyal foot soldier. Arthur and Eileen Hirsch are the King and Queen of Kit-Catdom and I'd like to take this opportunity to thank them in public for making me look so good.

PART IV

Recovery: For Professionals Only

CHAPTER 16

A License to Steal: Prices Slashed to Retail!

Dogs get licensed and so do drivers. Did you know that sellers get licensed, too? The first question Arthur Hirsch asked me when I queried him about doing business was, "Do you have a resale license?" I did. If I hadn't, we wouldn't be doing business today!

Why Be Licensed?

A reseller's license, also known as a seller's permit, is the key to a private club that allows its members to buy wholesale—in theory at least. Obtaining one is not only imperative in order to go into business, it's the first meaningful step in declaring yourself a professional. Nothing levels the playing field quicker than a seller's permit! Without it one can't compete effectively.

The good news is that a resale license costs nothing and is exceptionally easy to get. The bad news is that you're going to have to get your act together—using a seller's permit requires that you keep books like a corporation, and file taxes like one as well. Once you obtain a reseller's license from your state, the state will view you as an ongoing business operation. It will be incumbent upon you to collect state sales tax when appropriate and to file a special tax return once or more per year to remit the collected taxes to your state. In exchange, a resale license provides you with a tax exemption and sanctions you to buy wholesale goods from any corporation in America or worldwide. That's quite a tradeoff! Figure 16.1 shows what an application for a state seller's permit looks like in California.

After weeks of soul-searching and procrastination it took me less than five minutes to fill out the form. I downloaded form BOE-400-MIP, Application for Seller's Permit, from the State of California Board of Equalization Web site. It was an Adobe Acrobat (.pdf) file that took less than a minute to open. I compliment the State of California for being so high-tech.

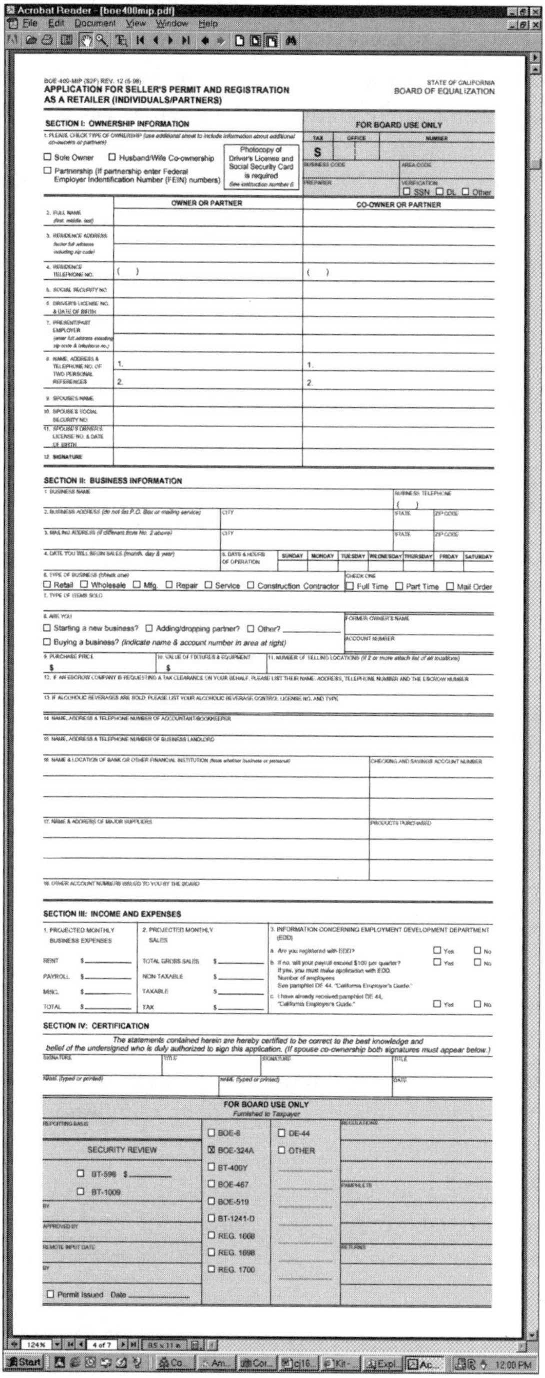
Acrobat Reader - [boe400mip.pdf]

File Edit Document View Window Help

BOE-400-MIP (S2F) REV. 12 (5-98)

STATE OF CALIFORNIA
BOARD OF EQUALIZATION

APPLICATION FOR SELLER'S PERMIT AND REGISTRATION AS A RETAILER (INDIVIDUALS/PARTNERS)

SECTION I: OWNERSHIP INFORMATION

1. PLEASE CHECK TYPE OF OWNERSHIP *(use additional sheet to include information about additional co-owners or partners)*

☐ Sole Owner ☐ Husband/Wife Co-ownership

☐ Partnership (If partnership enter Federal Employer Indentification Number (FEIN) numbers)

Photocopy of Driver's License and Social Security Card is required *See instruction number 6*

FOR BOARD USE ONLY: TAX S | OFFICE | NUMBER | BUSINESS CODE | AREA CODE | PREPARER | VERIFICATION ☐ SSN ☐ DL ☐ Other

	OWNER OR PARTNER	CO-OWNER OR PARTNER
2. FULL NAME *(first, middle, last)*		
3. RESIDENCE ADDRESS *(enter full address including zip code)*		
4. RESIDENCE TELEPHONE NO.	( )	( )
5. SOCIAL SECURITY NO.		
6. DRIVER'S LICENSE NO. & DATE OF BIRTH		
7. PRESENT/PAST EMPLOYER *(enter full address including zip code & telephone no.)*		
8. NAME, ADDRESS & TELEPHONE NO. OF TWO PERSONAL REFERENCES	1. 2.	1. 2.
9. SPOUSE'S NAME		
10. SPOUSE'S SOCIAL SECURITY NO.		
11. SPOUSE'S DRIVER'S LICENSE NO. & DATE OF BIRTH		
12. SIGNATURE		

SECTION II: BUSINESS INFORMATION

1. BUSINESS NAME — BUSINESS TELEPHONE ( )
2. BUSINESS ADDRESS *(do not list P.O. Box or mailing service)* — CITY — STATE — ZIP CODE
3. MAILING ADDRESS *(if different from No. 2 above)* — CITY — STATE — ZIP CODE
4. DATE YOU WILL BEGIN SALES *(month, day & year)*
5. DAYS & HOURS OF OPERATION: SUNDAY | MONDAY | TUESDAY | WEDNESDAY | THURSDAY | FRIDAY | SATURDAY
6. TYPE OF BUSINESS *(check one)* ☐ Retail ☐ Wholesale ☐ Mfg. ☐ Repair ☐ Service ☐ Construction Contractor — CHECK ONE ☐ Full Time ☐ Part Time ☐ Mail Order
7. TYPE OF ITEMS SOLD
8. ARE YOU ☐ Starting a new business? ☐ Adding/dropping partner? ☐ Other? ______ ☐ Buying a business? *(indicate name & account number in area at right)* — FORMER OWNER'S NAME — ACCOUNT NUMBER
9. PURCHASE PRICE $ — 10. VALUE OF FIXTURES & EQUIPMENT $ — 11. NUMBER OF SELLING LOCATIONS *(if 2 or more attach list of all locations)*
12. IF AN ESCROW COMPANY IS REQUESTING A TAX CLEARANCE ON YOUR BEHALF, PLEASE LIST THEIR NAME, ADDRESS, TELEPHONE NUMBER AND THE ESCROW NUMBER
13. IF ALCOHOLIC BEVERAGES ARE SOLD, PLEASE LIST YOUR ALCOHOLIC BEVERAGE CONTROL LICENSE NO. AND TYPE
14. NAME, ADDRESS & TELEPHONE NUMBER OF ACCOUNTANT/BOOKKEEPER
15. NAME, ADDRESS & TELEPHONE NUMBER OF BUSINESS LANDLORD
16. NAME & LOCATION OF BANK OR OTHER FINANCIAL INSTITUTION *(state whether business or personal)* — CHECKING AND SAVINGS ACCOUNT NUMBER
17. NAME & ADDRESS OF MAJOR SUPPLIERS — PRODUCTS PURCHASED
18. OTHER ACCOUNT NUMBERS ISSUED TO YOU BY THE BOARD

SECTION III: INCOME AND EXPENSES

1. PROJECTED MONTHLY BUSINESS EXPENSES: RENT $____ PAYROLL $____ MISC. $____ TOTAL $____

2. PROJECTED MONTHLY SALES: TOTAL GROSS SALES $____ NON TAXABLE $____ TAXABLE $____ TAX $____

3. INFORMATION CONCERNING EMPLOYMENT DEVELOPMENT DEPARTMENT (EDD)
a. Are you registered with EDD? ☐ Yes ☐ No
b. If no, will your payroll exceed $100 per quarter? ☐ Yes ☐ No
If yes, you must make application with EDD.
Number of employees
See pamphlet DE 44, "California Employer's Guide."
c. I have already received pamphlet DE 44, "California Employer's Guide." ☐ Yes ☐ No

SECTION IV: CERTIFICATION

The statements contained herein are hereby certified to be correct to the best knowledge and belief of the undersigned who is duly authorized to sign this application. (If spouse co-ownership both signatures must appear below.)

SIGNATURE — TITLE — SIGNATURE — TITLE
NAME *(typed or printed)* — NAME *(typed or printed)* — DATE

FOR BOARD USE ONLY
Furnished to Taxpayer

REPORTING BASIS — SECURITY REVIEW ☐ BT-598 $____ ☐ BT-1009 — BY — APPROVED BY — REMOTE INPUT DATE — BY — ☐ Permit Issued Date ____

☐ BOE-8 ☒ BOE-324A ☐ BT-400Y ☐ BOE-467 ☐ BOE-519 ☐ BT-1241-D ☐ REG. 1668 ☐ REG. 1698 ☐ REG. 1700

☐ DE-44 ☐ OTHER

REGULATIONS — PAMPHLETS — RETURNS

124% 4 of 7 8.5 x 11 in

Start Co... Am... Cor... cj16... Kir-... Expl... Ac... 12:00 PM

Figure 16.1 *California seller's permit application*

Who Needs a Seller's Permit?

According to the State of California, "If you sell taxable merchandise or provide a taxable service such as renting merchandise or fabrication labor, you must have a Seller's Permit. Wholesalers as well as retailers must have a separate permit for each place of business." The same basic rule applies in all states. In addition to filling out a simple two-page application I was required to supply photocopies of my Social Security card and my driver's license. I received my seller's permit eight days after submitting the application.

What Does Holding a Seller's Permit Entail?

When you obtain a seller's permit, you acquire valuable rights and privileges in exchange for additional responsibilities.

➤ You may purchase property for resale without paying tax. When you provide a vendor with a completed resale certificate, you are not required to pay sales tax on tangible personal property you purchase for resale. However, you can not use a resale certificate if you intend to use the property prior to or instead of selling it. If you intend to use the property, you must pay sales tax.

➤ You must keep adequate records to substantiate your sales, deductions reported on your returns, and any purchases you have made for your business. Records must be kept for four years.

➤ You must file returns. Tax returns must be filed on or before the last day of the month following your reporting period. You must file your return even if you did not sell any merchandise.

➤ You must pay taxes. As a seller, you must pay taxes on gross receipts from retail sales. However, you are allowed by law to be reimbursed by collecting the tax from your customers.

➤ You must notify the state if you move, change ownership of, or sell your business. Your permit is valid only at the address and for the type of ownership specified on the permit.

Prices Slashed to Retail!

There's a trendy clothing store on the outskirts of Beverly Hills that holds a twice-yearly sale. People come from miles around to get a break on the boutique's normally outrageous prices. A friend of mine and I arrived at seven o'clock in the morning on sale day and there was already a line stretching around the corner. The store wasn't even open yet! When the store did open, 50 customers at a time were allowed in; my buddy and I finally got inside about an hour and a half later. We went our own ways to check out the merchandise and met up again about twenty minutes later. Neither of us had purchased a thing. As the security guard let us out the door my pal glanced at me skeptically and exclaimed, "Prices slashed to retail!"

Wholeselling Exposed

I thought a seller's permit was a license to steal, all that would be necessary to conquer the Web! I'm a gadget freak and a computer geek. I know what sells and I had a plan! The moment I received my seller's permit I would apply for accounts with Ingram Micro and Merisel, two of the biggest wholesale distributors of electronics and computer components in the world. When you buy a brand name computer component or software program from a major Web site like Egghead it is often shipped from the warehouses of one of these two companies.

Visions of giant markups danced in my head! Ingram Micro and Merisel are the authorized distributors for everybody who's anyone in the computer industry. You name it—3Com, 3dfx, Adaptec, Adobe, Cisco, Compaq, Corel, Epson, Hewlett Packard, IBM, Iomega, Kensington, Kingston, Microsoft, NEC, Seagate, Symantec, Toshiba—the list goes on and on.

Compared with obtaining a seller's permit, opening an account with these two companies felt like enlisting in the CIA. Representatives of both organizations called to qualify me. One even had the audacity to suggest that the name of my Web site, Unique Boutique, didn't sound computerey enough. I'm certain that the only reason I got an account with either is that I claimed my main supplier was the other. In addition to being one another's biggest competitors, Merisel and Ingram Micro are arch rivals.

The following week my "Welcome Kits" arrived, one from each company. Inside were massive directories of every computer component known to man cataloged like names in a telephone book. Ingram Micro included a T-shirt. Not to be outdone, Merisel threw in a mouse pad. Their catalogs were almost identical, but Ingram Micro's was a bit thicker, coming in at over a thousand pages. I hardly gave them a second glance. It wasn't the catalogs I was interested in—it was my account number in their welcome letter that would enable me to access their Web sites so that I could determine the wholesale prices of the goods I wanted to sell.

The first time I logged on to Merisel's Web site I got giddy. I typed in my user name and password and the walls came tumbling down. "Welcome Michael Weber," pronounced the next screen. They knew me! I felt like a kid in a candy store. With hundreds of thousands of wholesale computer components at my fingertips I hardly knew where to begin! I impulsively conducted a search on an Epson Stylus 900 color printer because I'd recently purchased one for $330 including shipping from Club Computer and was curious about how much Merisel would have saved me. I waited with bated breath. There it was, an Epson Stylus 900 color printer. But something was radically wrong—it cost fifty or sixty bucks more than I paid, plus shipping!

Perhaps I was just using the site incorrectly, I thought. I hastily conducted a second search. I had recently upgraded my video card to a Diamond Viper V770 TNT2, bought from Egghead Computer for $149 including shipping. Coincidentally, the video card was drop-shipped to me directly from Merisel's warehouse! Once again, Merisel's price was considerably more than I paid. Would you believe $189? I got a queasy feeling in the pit of my stomach as I harkened back to my friend's words from that sale-day morn: "Prices slashed to retail!"

All Accounts Are Not Created Equal

I logged on to the Ingram Micro site and it was like déjà vu all over again. Their prices were virtually identical to Merisel's. I decided to light my calabash pipe and don my investigative reporter's hat. An experiment was required! I chose ten popular products and compared prices on the sites of Ingram Micro, Merisel, eBay, and using the CNET.com shopping bot. I searched each site on the same day. The prices from eBay reflected auctions that had already closed. To maintain fairness and consistency, on several occasions I threw out the lowest price on eBay and the shopping bot to be replaced by a price more commensurate and representative of the majority. Table 16.1 shows the results.

Table 16.1 The "Prices Slashed To Retail" Wholesale Experiment

Product	Ingram	Merisel	eBay	Shopping Bot
IBM ThinkPad 390X P3-450	$2,287.00	$2,212.84	$1625 used; $2175 new	$2161.95 Buy.com
Intel FSB 133 Pentium III P3 733 CPU	$381.00	$369.01	$225 new	$350.99 Egghead Software
Intel 18m CM Pentium III P3 733 CPU	$387.50	NA	$436 new	$352.99 Egghead Software
Microsoft Windows 2000 Pro	$244.15	$242.62	$187.50 new	$168 Advanced Vision Inc.
HP LaserJet 5000	$1,479.00	$1,427.15	$1126 demo	$1278 Infinity Micro
Adobe Photoshop 5.5	$503.00	$600.49	$305.00 new	$475.00 Page Computer
Creative Labs DTT2500 Desktop Theater	$262.00	$250.77	$167.50 new	$199.99 Solutions4-Sure.com
3Com—Palm Computing Palm V	$297.50	$353.69	$285.00 new (Palm Vx)	$274.99 Buy.com
Nikon Coolpix 990	$903.00	$868.08	$861.00 new	$826.00 Best Stop Digital
Toshiba Satellite 2180CDT	$1,220.00	$1,188.10	$940.00 new	$1098.95 PC Mall
TOTAL (Minus INTEL 18m CM)	$7,576.65	$7,512.75	$6,272.00	$6,833.87

What's wrong with this picture? In the aggregate, Merisel and Ingram Micro charged 17 percent more than the folks on eBay and 10 percent more than the shopping bot for ten identical products. Is it mere coincidence that Ingram Micro and Merisel's price differential for the ten items totals less than 1 percent? You can draw your own conclusions.

How can these companies claim to be wholesale distributors when their prices are uniformly above average? And if their prices are uniformly above average, why do the biggest sites on the Internet use Merisel and Ingram Micro as their mainline distributors? Do their largest customers get a price break or does Ingram Micro and Merisel charge all customers the same price? How is it that products drop-shipped from Ingram Micro and Merisel's warehouses and purchased through third parties like Egghead cost less for that product than Ingram Micro and Merisel charge directly? Inquiring minds want to know! I posed these questions to the gentlemen best equipped to answer: Kent Foster, president of Ingram Micro, and Dwight Steffensen and his predecessor, Ron Smith, presidents of Merisel.

I queried both companies on numerous occasions by e-mail, letter, and phone, identifying myself as an author with a company account. The query letters can be found on the *Confessions* CD-ROM under Corroboration. The query contained Table 16.1 and posed four questions.

1. Is it a coincidence that Ingram Micro and Merisel's price differential for the ten items totals less than 1%?

2. If your prices are uniformly above eBay and the shopping bot's, as it would appear, why do the biggest sites on the Internet use Merisel and Ingram Micro as their mainline distributors?

3. Do your largest customers get a price break or does Merisel/Ingram charge all customers the same price?

4. How is it that products drop-shipped from your warehouse and purchased through third parties like Egghead cost less than what you charge directly?

I'd like to report these companies were forthcoming with their answers, but alas, they weren't. They may feel that answering these questions is a breach of proprietary information. When I asked my account rep at one of these firms "how can third parties like Egghead charge less for products than you do for the same products drop-shipped from your warehouse?" the account rep cited "burn rate," the phenomenon discussed in Chapter 2. She said that some e-commerce sites sell products below wholesale to build large customer bases and impress Wall Street with inflated gross sales figures.

Judging from recent bankruptcies in the e-commerce sector like Value America she may be partially right, but there has to be more to these wholesale business operations than that. Ingram Micro and Merisel had months to reply to my questions but the best I could get out of either was "no comment."

What else can be garnered from the results of this experiment?

➤ **Buying from so-called wholesalers and distributors doesn't guarantee the lowest price.** Ingram Micro and Merisel combined didn't register one "lowest price" among the ten chosen items. Their prices were somewhat competitive on the IBM ThinkPad, the Intel Pentium CPU, the 3Com Palm V, and the Nikon Coolpix. One should look upon words like "wholesale" and "distributor" with skepticism. Sadly, in this day and age these words have been reduced to advertising slogans.

➤ **There are no formulas.** When it comes to obtaining the lowest wholesale price it's imperative that you shop around. The shopping bot was the way to go on the ThinkPad, Windows 2000, the Palm V, and the Nikon Coolpix. eBay scored the lowest price on the Pentium CPU, the LaserJet 5000, Adobe PhotoShop, the Creative Labs Desktop Theater, and the Toshiba Satellite. One exception to this rule may be in the aggregate; over time, Internet auctions possibly offer the lowest price, at least when it comes to computer components.

➤ **Internet auctions and shopping bots are legitimate wholesale sources.** Many professional auctioneers have confided that Internet auctions and shopping bots are their primary source of merchandise. One can only guess how many items are recycled goods from previous auctions. When in doubt, e-mail an auctioneer your questions before bidding on his item. I once bid on a "retail" version of Corel Draw that I had to return to the auctioneer after discovering it was an OEM version missing two clip art CD-ROMs and the manual. When bidding on an allegedly new product, make certain it is sealed in its box and comes with the full registration and manuals. Don't be shy! Use e-mail as a truth detector.

Ante Up

Should the previous experiment dissuade you from getting a seller's permit? Not if you're serious about selling professionally. A seller's permit is your credential, a mandatory accouterment to your business identity. And to be honest, I came to realize that markups in the electronics and computer component sector are razor thin, and the competition is cutthroat. Many products can sustain a hundred percent markup and more.

Most manufacturers won't do business with you unless you have a seller's permit. On the other hand, obtaining a resale license opens you up to the scrutiny of your state. It obliges you to collect and remit sales tax and file a special tax return. My best advice—don't open a can of worms unless you intend to go fishing!

CHAPTER 17

Finding Your Own Niche: Fishing Around

- ➤ Window Shopping for Inspiration and Profit
- ➤ Unearthing Saleable Products
- ➤ Finding the Right Pitch
- ➤ Capo di Tutti-You're the Boss

By arming yourself with a seller's permit you've leveled the playing field: from the manufacturers' standpoint there's no difference between you and millions of other retailers and resellers vying for their products. Of course you're *more* welcome if you're *Wal-Mart* than if you're *Walter Martin*, but putting that aside, you've evolved from an entity into an account. Congratulations. They covet your business! But who are *they* and where do you find them?

Window Shopping for Inspiration and Profit

You're surrounded by opportunity when it comes to finding products to sell. The best place to start looking is right in your own neighborhood. Hit the bricks, go window shopping! Canvass the local boutiques and mall. Imagine what you see in the window inside the framework of an Internet auction. What would sell? If something strikes your fancy step inside the store and check it out. Look at the label. Is it a name brand? Is it searchable? Who's the manufacturer? Where is the plant located? How much does the item retail for? Jot it all down in the notepad you brought along.

Have you been approached by a salesperson yet? If not, approach them. Be friendly! Sales staff are usually only too happy to let you to pick their brains, so fire away! First, introduce yourself and find out who you're talking to. Then start digging. Is the product a hot seller? Is the model old or new? Does it ever go on sale? At what price? Does the store give quantity discounts? Does it have a wholesale division? Does it have a Web site? If not, would the store be interested in a Web site? Mention that you sell products on the Internet like the one you're discussing, but don't get more specific than that. Ask for the manager or owner's name and jot it down on the back of the store's business card along with the salesperson's name. Now wish them a pleasant day and move along to the next shop window.

I recently discovered a smashing product, magnetic stud earrings, exactly this way. A powerful hidden magnet locks them invisibly to the ear lobe. They retail for $6.50 a pair but the store has a wholesale division. I contacted it and was quoted a price of .85 cents per pair with a $100 minimum order. I wasn't limited to purchasing earrings, either. The wholesale division has hundreds of hip items, all dirt cheap. In addition to discovering a new product to sell, at the end of the day I found a super new wholesale resource.

The $18 Corporate Makeover

Now that you're in business it's time to start thinking about a business card. It would be a nice touch if you could hand the salesclerk your business card and suggest he pass it along to the owner because you might be able to help generate revenue for the store. A business card opens a plethora of doors by advertising your legitimacy. In addition to your name, address, phone number, and fax, it should contain your e-mail address, Web site URL, and the name of your company spelled out in big, bold letters. Since you most likely don't have a Web site yet, I advise you to hold off on printing your business card until you've read the next chapter, which details how to obtain a Web site for free.

In the interim, do some homework. Come up with a catchy name for your Web site and company and design your business card so it reflects and highlights that name. Lay it out in your favorite graphic design program or download a business card design utility under Software on the *Confessions* CD-ROM. Next, locate a printer in your local Yellow Pages who advertises business cards as a specialty. You should be able to get 500 business cards printed in raised black and white letters (known in the printing trade as thermography) on a reasonably thick card stock for under twenty bucks. Let your fingers do the walking until you come up with a few alternatives and then drive to those shops to check out their printing quality. Describe what you're after and check out their samples. If you see something you like in stock, stick with their design—it will be much easier for them to replicate. Be sure you communicate clearly with the printer before you proceed—500 business cards are going to last you an awfully long time!

Unearthing Saleable Products

There are hot products with your name on them out there somewhere. If you haven't found them yet, don't despair—your search has just begun. Numerous other methods for locating the product of your dreams are at your disposal.

Using the B-To-B Yellow Pages

The best way to locate wholesale goods within driving distance is with your local Ma Bell Business-to-Business Yellow Pages. It's free and it's an incredibly powerful resource! Call your local phone company and ask for a copy. Use it like an armchair general. Sit down and prop it on your knee. It's massive. With a pencil and pad in one hand and a cordless phone in the other, let your imagination run wild! Whatever you can dream of selling can be found in those Yellow Pages! Open the book to any page at random. Take notes. Call around, but don't get frustrated. Many manufacturers are Mom-and-Pop operations and you'll often encounter a recorded message. Always be polite and ask them to return your call.

Searching the Liquidators

There's nothing like a product that costs next to nothing and sells like hot cakes after you mark it up 1000 percent! Liquidators differ from wholesalers, distributors, and manufacturers in a critical way: they sell goods for pennies on the dollar. Liquidators are the back door to the bargain basement of American commerce. What didn't sell on Main Street will eventually sell here. Liquidators buy goods by the cargo container and sell them by the pallet. They aren't interested in quality, they're only interested in price.

There are numerous treasures buried among the trash but you have to go digging! Several liquidators have Web sites, so this can be done in the comfort of your own living room. I've done more rummaging around these sites than I'd like to admit. I find some of the merchandise that people get stuck with nothing short of mind-boggling. Most liquidators have a minimum purchase requirement ranging from $100 to $250, so buyer beware! You only have thumbnail pictures and brief descriptions to go on and all sales are final.

One of the best resources for liquidators is contained in Profit-Master. You'll find a copy on the *Confessions* CD-ROM under Profit-Master. Open TURORIAL.HTM, click Buying and Selling, and—while you're online—check out the listings under Master Wholesale Web sites.

The Thomas Register

The *Thomas Register of American Manufacturers* is an invaluable resource for locating wholesale products. It presently lists 156,914 companies that manufacture goods in 63,699 different product categories. The *Register* now lists Canadian companies as well so its full name is a bit of a misnomer.

The *Thomas Register* is available in almost every library in America. Before the Internet a trip to the library was required, but now the Register is accessible online, at http://www.thomasregister.com. Registration is free. All the companies and product categories are searchable, and 7,782 of the companies have Web sites with direct links to the Thomas site. Happy hunting!

Search Engines

Nothing cuts to the chase quicker than an Internet search engine—if you know what you're looking for. The rap on search engines is that there are so many listings it's hard to separate the wheat from the chaff. This may apply when it comes to simple searches but an advanced search should remedy this.

Most search engines support some combination of following advanced options:

> ➤ **Double-quoted phrases (" ")**. For example, type in **"john lennon"** and not simply john lennon. Putting quotes around a set of words will find only those results that match the words in that exact sequence.

> ➤ **Enforced Term Operators (+/-)**. For example, type in **music +"john lennon" –beatles**. Attaching a plus sign (+) to a word requires that the word be found in all of the search results. Attaching a minus sign (-) in front of a word requires that the word not be found in any of the search results.

> ➤ **Boolean language** (and, or, not). For example, type in **music and "john lennon" and not beatles**.

You may improve your results by using these advanced search techniques, but not all engines support them. Try out different approaches to see what works best for you. Experiment with the words *wholesale* or *discount* in your search string. It doesn't always work but if it does you'll hit the jackpot!

For a complete list of search engines click on Find Anything in Profit-Master or Search Engines on the *Confessions* CD-ROM.

CNET offers another fine service, a master search engine that searches 700 others—check it out at http://www.search.com.

Surplus Auctions

Surplus auctions differ from Internet auctions in that the seller is the site itself. You can't list items for sale, you can only bid on them. The bargains are fantastic, however, typically 50 percent to 75 percent below retail. Two of my favorite golden oldies are http://www.onsale.com, the surplus outlet for Egghead, and http://www.ubid.com.

Mercata.com

The latest and greatest incarnation of the surplus auction yet may be http://www.mercata.com. By taking advantage of the power of the Internet, Mercata brings shoppers together so that they can pool their purchasing power to achieve major savings.

Mercata calls each auction a "group purchase," a time-limited buying opportunity that allows you to join other online shoppers to drive prices down. The more people who decide to purchase a specific item, the lower the price. It's a win-win situation. You benefit with increased savings and manufacturers and distributors benefit by selling more products. The most exciting aspect of a Mercata auction is the way the prices lower regularly. Through the site's patented technology, the price drops as more people participate and you're provided with constant updates on the progress of the group purchase.

Trade Shows and Flea Markets

Hands down, the best place I know of to discover great wholesale products and contacts is at a trade show. Where else can you compare thousands of wholesale products side by side and embark on relationships with the people who manufacture and distribute them? The most profitable trade shows to attend are gift, boutique, fashion, housewares, electronics, novelty, general merchandise, and accessories. You won't find too many hot products at Widget Expo!

Of course, trade shows are few and far between and you probably need to live near a big city with a large convention center to attend one without spending an arm and a leg. Check out the Web site of your nearest convention center and search the upcoming events schedule.

Conversely, the biggest waste of time I've found in terms of locating great bargains is at commercial flea markets. Many of the best items can be found on the Internet for less and a majority of the rest is trash. The one exception to this rule is if you're a collector. If you know what to look for, that trash might turn out to contain your treasure.

Internet Auctions and Shopping Bots

The experiment in the last chapter is proof positive that Internet auctions and shopping bots are invaluable wholesale resources. The experiment also proves there are no definitive formulas when it comes to unearthing the lowest price. In the final analysis, great markups result from due diligence and exhaustive comparison shopping.

Finding the Right Pitch

All of your hard work will pay off. One day you'll clutch a product in your hands that could earn you thousands of dollars. When it happens, a strange mix of trepidation and exhilaration will overcome you—relief followed by uncertainty. How should you proceed?

It's time to take stock. You didn't arrive here by accident. You knew what to look for. You also have a great deal of expertise in the field of Internet sales— you sold hundreds, maybe thousands of dollars worth of merchandise in a very short time. Look at how many auctions you ran and how many HTML ads you've created. That's not chopped liver.

Walk a mile in the moccasins of your average small or medium-sized manufacturer. The majority wouldn't know the Internet from a hair net! They're too busy churning out products and shipping orders. The small number who are Internet savvy certainly don't have time to fiddle around with Internet auctions. The quality of your pitch will ultimately determine the value of your deal, so get your rap down before you start blabbering!

Invest in Their Success

You're not just some new account coming in over the transom. You're willing to invest cold, hard cash to advertise the manufacturer's product to millions of people on the Web. Make that clear in your first sentence. There's no need to embellish when it comes to the subject of Internet auctions because it's a hot topic—everybody's heard of eBay.

Be honest. You don't know if their product will sell or not. The important thing is that you believe in it enough to *test market* it. It won't be worth the manufacturer's time or your investment unless you can sell a few dozen a week. You'll never know until you try. That's all you're suggesting.

Ask and Ye Shall Receive

Now it's time to allow the manufacturers to walk a mile in your moccasins. Once upon a time they were new in business, too, and along the way someone no doubt gave them a helping hand. You're now where they were. Ask for their advice or assistance!

People are often reluctant to ask for help because doing so seems to shift power to the helper. Asking for help is in reality a most empowering and underrated business technique, because it can engender empathy. People do enjoy providing help to others—if they don't have to sacrifice *too* much of their time or money. It makes them feel good. The key is asking! This is one of the best kept secrets on earth.

Can You Get the Lowest Price with No Minimum Order?

To sell an item at a competitive price you must pay rock-bottom wholesale. Most manufacturers have minimum orders with sliding price scales for higher quantities. You want the minimum order waived and the lowest wholesale price. And you don't want to pay for inventory until you have orders. If you can persuade a manufacturer to make concessions on either of these points you're in business! If somebody asks why he should give you a break, answer "because you have nothing to lose!" Agree on price and payment terms ASAP. Strike while the iron is hot! Last but not least, make certain the manufacturer has enough inventory in stock to fulfill your orders if the product does take off.

Will They Drop-Ship?

If you find a manufacturer willing to drop-ship, you just hit the jackpot! The manufacturer has to ship the product somewhere. Why can't it be directly to your customers instead of to you? Of course, you'll make it worth their while. What do they think would be a fair handling fee? A buck or two, somewhere in between? Whatever they ask is worth the price of not having to pack and unpack inventory and endure long lines in the post office. Manufacturers who drop-ship make life a joy. Get off the phone immediately, before they reconsider!

Put Your Money Where Your Mouth Is

The only way your product has a fair chance of seeing the light of day is if you list it as a featured auction in the appropriate category or categories. Doing so will ensure your headline appears on the front page of that category. Table 17.1 lays out some fees associated with placement and marketing.

Table 17.1 Big Three Auction Site Fees

Feature	Amazon	eBay	Yahoo!
Featured on site home page	N/A	$99.95	N/A
Featured in category day and up	$0.05 day and up	$14.95	$0.10
Boldface	$2	$2	$2
Gallery	N/A	.25 and up	N/A
Special icons	N/A	$1	$1
Insertion fee	$0.10	$0.25 to $2	Free
Cut on a $25 sale	5 percent	5 percent	None

It pays to advertise, so don't be chintzy! I typically pay $400 or $500 a month to run my Internet auctions. The higher the bill the happier I am because big bills signify that my products are selling. I'll feature a hot product in multiple categories without hesitation. Cat lovers won't find my Kit-Cat clocks in Home Furnishings, so I feature them in Cat Collectibles, too.

Regarding the pennies-a-day featured auctions available on Amazon and Yahoo!, I'm afraid you get what you pay for. Today I checked Amazon for every featured auction on the site and came up with grand total of 147. How do you spell nosedive? My best advice is to pass on Amazon and Yahoo! when it comes to featured auctions and bet the farm on eBay.

Capo di Tutti-You're the Boss

Accountability is the price of freedom! The wholesale resources and hypothetical deals discussed in this chapter are merely the tip of the iceberg, suggested starting points, and directions to explore. The difference between you and that salesclerk slaving away fifty hours a week is that you're the boss. Good deals don't grow on trees—go out, seek, and find them. The onus is on you to be the Capo of your own regime. To succeed you must seize the initiative!

The Web Is Your Oyster: Open a Web Site and They Will Click!

- ➢ Maintaining Multiple Sites
- ➢ A Web Site Is Your Best Advertisement
- ➢ Be the Webmaster of Your Own Destiny
- ➢ Making Yourself Known on the Web

In the future everyone will have a Web site for fifteen minutes.
—*Andy Warhol (through a medium)*

I had one customer, a prince from Riyadh, who loved to smoke cigars. He ordered a ton of smoking accessories on my Web site. One day he called long distance to thank me and mentioned in passing that if he was ever caught with the paraphernalia I sent him he could get his pinky finger cut off. In all conscience, I had to stop selling to him. This was more than a humanitarian consideration: I didn't want to get in trouble for exporting contraband, and this guy wanted to become my Persian Gulf distributor!

Maintaining Multiple Sites

Having been born with the last name of Weber I guess it's inevitable that I'd have several Web sites. I presently maintain six. Four are unique and two are mirror sites. I don't contribute a single dime toward the support of any—they run on good faith and elbow grease!

I designed and programmed each site—with the exception of my online store in the ICAT Mall—from scratch, using Front Page 2000 or FP Express. As a Webmaster, I'm proud to say that these sites run themselves. Each has the capacity to produce revenue even when I'm sleeping or walking my dog. Think about that!

➤ **http://zenweb.webjump.com**. Zenweb Creative Services is an Internet advertising agency offering Web site design, graphics, and ad campaigns. It also serves an electronic portfolio. (See Figure 18.1.)

➤ **http://unboutique.webjump.com**. Unique Boutique is an e-commerce site offering Kit-Cat clocks, lighters, cigar accessories, and humidors. It processes secure credit card orders via a built-in virtual shopping cart. (See Figure 18.2.)

➤ **http://members.aol.com/urlegant/default.htm**. This Kit-Cat Shopping Cart is where my Internet auction winners are directed to place secure credit card orders. (See Figure 18.3.)

➤ **http://www.icatmall.com/urlegant**. URLegant Kit-Cat Klocks can be found in the ICAT Mall, a Cyberspace shopping mall owned and operated by Intel. The store was prefabricated using ICAT's proprietary software in less than an hour. I was grandfathered in to a lifetime lease before ICAT started charging $19.95 and up per month for this service. The site processes secure credit card orders via a built-in virtual shopping cart. Because it was pre-fabbed this site is an eyesore so I'll spare you.

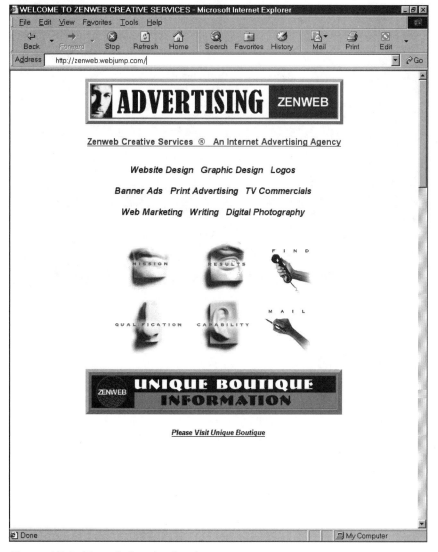

Figure 18.1 *Zenweb Creative Services*

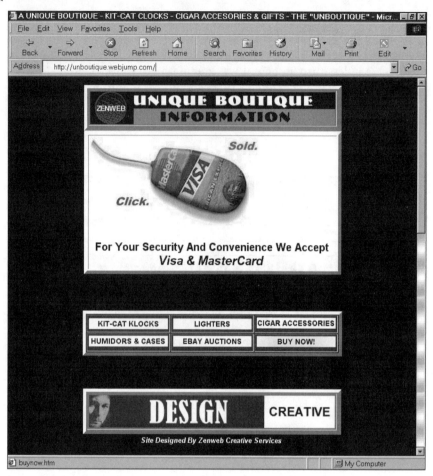

Figure 18.2 *Unique Boutique, the* un*boutique*

Name Value

These sites are mine but I don't *own* them. By the time you read this book it will have a Web site too. I won't own it either! I'll own its *domain name*. My dictionary defines *domain* as "A territory over which rule or control is exerted." This is one of the most apt descriptions in the annals of computerese. The territory over which rule or control is exerted on the Internet is disk space on a Web server.

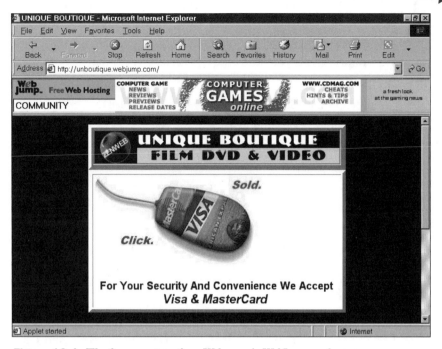

Figure 18.4 *The frame on top of my Web page is WebJump real estate*

WebJump offers the following, per site, for no monthly fee and no setup charge:

➤ 25MB disk space

➤ Unlimited bandwidth

➤ Round-the-clock technical support

Using a Monthly-fee Web Host

I'm not promising that my Web sites will forever be hosted on free servers. Nor am I necessarily recommending that you go that route. You *do* get more by paying for a host, and you may decide that the price is worth it.

By way of example, Webhosting.Com, one of the world's premiere Web hosts, provides the following (per site), for as little as $19.95 a month:

➤ 125MB of disk storage

➤ 99.9 percent up-time guarantee

➤ 25 POP3 e-mail addresses

➤ 24-hour FTP access

➤ Unlimited auto-responders

➤ MS Front Page support

➤ 25 FTP accounts

➤ Unlimited e-mail aliases

➤ Real audio and video support

➤ Unlimited data transfer or hits

➤ Web control panel

➤ Site builder

Be the Webmaster of Your Own Destiny

A Web site is more than an adjunct to your auctions. It's an enterprise in itself. Orders from as far away as Australia, Japan, Saudi Arabia, and Germany have been placed on my site. In any given week my Web site produces more revenue than my auctions. And I haven't yet promoted it to the hilt because I'm just getting the hang of doing that.

Having a Web site nobody can find is like having no Web site at all! You, as an auctioneer, have a tremendous advantage over the average person launching a site. You have the marketing muscle of eBay, Amazon, and Yahoo! behind you. Your Web site is two clicks away from millions of potential customers! The first click is on your auction headline. The second click is on the banner ad at the bottom of your auction, which links shoppers directly to your Web site in a separate browser.

Commercials on the Internet

A *banner ad* is the Internet equivalent of a television commercial. Banner ads conform to a universal standard:

➤ 468×60 pixels

➤ GIF file format

➤ Small file size (10K to 15K maximum)

➤ Animation (optional)

Figure 18.5 *A 25-cent backdoor advertisement to your Web site*

If you surf the Web, you've seen thousands of banner ads. Once you launch your Web site, it's almost mandatory that you get one too. Personally, I like to create my own animated banner GIFs from scratch using Corel Photo-Paint, but you don't have to go to all the trouble. I searched ZDNET.com using the keyword "banner" this morning and got fifty-two hits on shareware or freeware banner-making programs. Click "Banner Makers" under Software on the *Confessions* CD-ROM for download links or conduct your own search on ZDNET.com.

I've tried Banner Factory, Banner Maker Professional, and Goetz Banner, and can recommend all three.

Run Your Banner up the Flagpole

The procedure for including a banner ad in your auction is virtually identical to inserting any GIF or JPG image. First, insert a hyperlink to the URL of your Web site in the HTML code of your auction ad. Don't forget to include the TARGET'"_BLANK" reference so that your Web site opens in a separate browser Window.

Here's how it works:

```
HREF' "HTTP://UNBOUTIQUE.WEBJUMP.COM"
TARGET' "_BLANK"><IMG
```

Next, insert the address of the FTP space where your banner GIF will be stored. The code looks like the following—with your own URL and GIF, of course:

```
SRC' "HTTP://MEMBERS.AOL.COM/ZENWEB/UBMARBLEBANNER4BIT.GIF"
```

Last, upload your banner GIF from your computer to your FTP space before listing your auction. That's all there is to it!

Making Yourself Known on the Web

With a Web site and a banner GIF, a world of possibilities opens for you. You can join an affiliate program with an Internet powerhouse like Amazon.com and then sell its wares on your Web site for a commission. You can join a banner network like Link Exchange, in which other banners appear on your site in exchange for your banner appearing elsewhere on the Web. You can submit your site to hundreds of Internet search engines. You can even pay to advertise your banner on other Web sites for as little as $50.

Affiliate Programs

An *affiliate program* allows you to ride the coattails of one of the big boys. It is a contractual agreement between you and a big company—like American Greetings, Barnes and Noble, Fogdog Sports, hardwarestreet.com, mothernature.com, art.com, or Amazon.com—to hawk their products on your Web site for a commission. The commissions generally range between 2.5 percent and 5 percent—chump-change! However, one program, XOOM.com, triples and even quintuples the going rate by offering commissions ranging between 15 percent and 25 percent. Its affiliate home page, http://www.xoom.com/xan/, invites you to "Wear Your Bathrobe To Work" every day! Click Affiliate Programs under Marketing on the *Confessions* CD-ROM for links.

Affiliate programs have provided one of the best lessons about the inner workings of the Internet that I've ever experienced. My first Web site was the all-affiliate site displayed in Figure 18.6, a glorified version of Amazon.com with a smidgen of Art.com and Beyond.com thrown in for good measure.

Figure 18.6 *My first Web site was this now defunct all-affiliate Web site.*

The procedure for placing a sponsor's product on your site is relatively simple. The sponsor gives you a few lines of HTML code, including your affiliate number and the product's SKU, its ID. You embed that code into a page on your Web site.

In theory, shoppers log on to your site and see a picture (hosted by the sponsor) of a product they like. They click on the image and are linked to the sponsor's site, and you collect a commission if the shopper places an order. Fat chance! I emphasize "in theory" because my twelve-page, all-affiliate Web site didn't earn a dime after taking dozens of man-hours to create. In summation, affiliate programs provided a lesson on the inner workings of the Internet by teaching me how not to waste my precious time!

This isn't to say affiliate programs can't provide limited benefits. I consider the Amazon.com search box, shown in Figure 18.7 an extremely beneficial resource, for example. My customers can search Amazon for any book, tape, CD, or anything else on their site. If the customer buys something as a result of the search I supposedly collect a commission. It's never happened. I consider providing an Amazon search box a public service, like a pay phone.

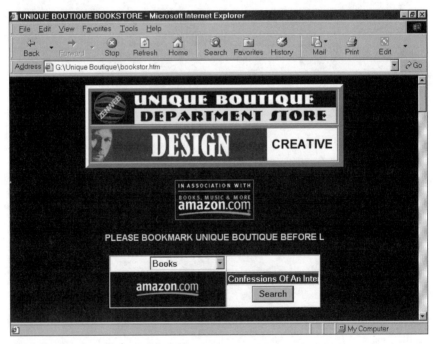

Figure 18.7 *You can search Amazon.com from one of my Web sites*

Banner Networks

Banner networks are terrific for the companies who own and operate them. But like affiliate programs, I consider them a tremendous waste of a Web-master's time. Banner networks sound good in theory. You embed the network's HTML code into your home page, and rotating banner ads for different Web sites will appear. Customers who click on a banner are transported to that site and the banner network reciprocates by placing your banner on another site.

My question is why would you want your customers to leave your site to go somebody else's? Another thing I don't like about banner networks is that they contain bots, complicated HTML components that retard your home page's loading speed.

Search Engine Submission

We're getting warmer! Remember that having a Web site nobody can find is like having no Web site at all. You want everybody to be able to find your Web site, even your worst enemies. Why shouldn't they be envious?

Nine out of ten Web surfers use a search engine to find what they're looking for. In addition to Yahoo!, Excite, Lycos, Alta Vista, AOL, MSN, Ask Jeeves, Northern Light, Go.com, and Goto.com there are hundreds of other search engines on the Internet. If your Web site doesn't come up in the first five hits of any given search you might as well be selling earmuffs in Miami. The top five Web sites get 90 percent of the click-throughs in any given search!

You can edge out richer, larger, mightier competitors simply by outmaneuvering them in an Internet search. Becoming a search engine top dog isn't rocket science: the investment in time and money is larger than the learning curve.

Search engines use software indexing agents—robots and spiders that constantly "crawl" the Internet in search of new or updated Web Pages. They essentially go from URL to URL until they have visited every Web site on the Internet. Each search engine examines a particular site to see if it meets specific criteria. The more criteria a Web site meets, the higher its position in a given search.

Each search engine analyzes a site's various elements. Web sites that take advantage of the following techniques generally obtain the highest rankings.

> ➤ **Title.** Use keywords in the title of your home page to make it as descriptive as possible. When visiting your site, an agent will first go to the <TITLE> tag. The <TITLE> tag is what a browser will display in the title bar. Instead of <TITLE> ACME as the title of ACME's

home page, <TITLE> ACME: Telescope Maker to the Stars is far more descriptive—it includes more words that are apt to show up in a search.

➤ **Meta Tags.** <META> tags enable you to provide extensive detail about the content of your Web site and thereby impose greater control over how your pages are indexed. Not all search engines make use of <META> tags, but adding these tags to your pages will make them more accessible to search engines that do.

The basic <META> tag syntax is:

➤ `<META NAME' "DESCRIPTION" content'"`a health and fitness center located in Atlanta">

➤ `<META NAME' "KEYWORDS" content'"`running, weight control, nutrition, aerobics, cholesterol, Georgia">

For detailed instructions on the use of <META> tags and other Web site tips click Webmaster Tools on the *Confessions* CD-ROM.

Get Ready for Prime-Time

Your Web site isn't ready for prime time until you do everything in your power to make it searchable. There are a couple of ways to skin this Kit-Cat (pardon the pun), namely a *search engine submission service* or *search engine submission software*. Essentially, for an initial investment of between $60 to $125, they do the same thing in the same way. You fill in information, which works as an adjunct to the <META> tag describing your Web site and the products or services you provide. The submission software or service then submits your Web site, automatically, to four-hundred-some-odd search engines, including all of the major Web portals. This process requires patience; Yahoo!, for example, can take up to eight weeks to list a site after it's been submitted. Once your site is listed, the service or software then checks the site's search engine rating and helps fine-tune its <META> tag to bump it up.

Submission software costs a bit more up front, but most submission services base their fees on a one-year renewable license—therefore over the long haul the service could end up costing you more. In addition, there's no restriction on the number of URLs one can submit with software, whereas a service charges more to list additional URLs. For these reasons, I recommend submission software over a submission service. In a pinch, either does the trick!

The Typical Prices for a one-year submission service license are as follows:

> ➤ $59 for 2 URLs (minimum license)
> ➤ $125 for 5 URLs
> ➤ $200 for 10 URLs
> ➤ $300 for 20 URLs
> ➤ $500 for 40 URLs

For $20 a month you can test market a combination of site submission and banner advertising. Here's what Microsoft's B-CENTRAL.com offers:

> ➤ 10 URLs listed on up to 400 search engines
> ➤ 5,000 banner ads per month on MSN'S network
> ➤ 5,000 e-mail messages per month to your customer database

Banner Advertising

The formula for a successful Web site is *hits* × *sales* = $. Once you've optimized your site's search engine ranking and it is turning a profit, it's time to reinvest some proceeds in banner advertising. I'm not talking about a banner network. I'm talking about paying for impressions of your banner ad on targeted Web sites. Following are rates for targeted Internet advertising from Smartage.com and its main competitor, Link Exchange.

SMARTAGE.com:

> ➤ $500 for 29,000 banner ad impressions
> ➤ $1,000 for 67,000 banner ad impressions
> ➤ $2,000 for 138,000 banner ad impressions

Link Exchange:

> ➤ (Special 2 For 1 Price) $8.00 per 1,000 impressions
> ➤ $50 for 3,000 banner ad impressions
> ➤ $150 for 9,500 × 2 = 19,000 banner ad impressions
> ➤ $300 for 19,500 × 2 = 39,000 banner ad impressions
> ➤ $600 for 40,000 × 2 = 80,000 banner ad impressions
> ➤ $1000 for 67,500 × 2 = 135,000 banner ad impressions

The next time you see some flashy animated banner on the Web, think to yourself, "That could be me." In reality, only a few hundred bucks separates you from the big time. Open a Web site and they will click!

The Merchant of Visa: The Buck Stops Here

In cyberspace, no one can hear the sound of a cash register ringing! Payment has always been the biggest bottleneck in any Internet transaction. As the educator and writer Marshall McLuhan stated way back in as 1971, "Money is the poor man's credit card." McLuhan envisioned electronic commerce as the currency of the future even before the invention of the Internet or the personal computer. He sure earned his stripes as a visionary.

Recently, the personal check has begun to go the way of the dodo. Only a year or so ago it was the primary form of Internet auction payment for those who didn't want to spring for the old standbys, money orders or cashier's checks. Several viable alternates have since surfaced.

> **Online escrow.** Online escrow works backwards. The buyer places funds in the care of an escrow service. The seller then ships the goods to the buyer. Only after the buyer approves does the seller receive the cash, after the escrow service takes its cut. It works, but it's clumsy. If you bid on an expensive oil painting and want to check on its authenticity, online escrow is feasible. Otherwise, forget about it. Online escrow is the only thing I know that's a bigger pain in the neck than a personal check.

> **PayPal and BillPoint.** PayPal and BillPoint are the Dr. Jekyll and Mr. Hyde of the e-pay revolution. They're virtually identical in form and function. The registered buyer pays by credit card and the registered seller authorizes the electronic transmittal of those funds into a specified account. The only real difference is that PayPal is absolutely *free* while BillPoint charges through the nose—39 cents for transactions of $9.99 and under, and 39 cents plus another 3.9 percent for transactions of $10 or more. These are exorbitant rates by any merchant account standard. I'm sorry to report that eBay is pushing BillPoint. Thumbs down! I give PayPal two enthusiastic thumbs up!

> **Credit cards.** The Cadillac of payment methods. To accept credit cards, however, a seller must first obtain a merchant account.

Merchant Accounts and Credit Cards

The first month I accepted credit cards my Internet auction sales tripled! By the end of that month I had recouped my initial investment in the merchant account, $465. The cost was a big lump to swallow up front, but few investments pay off so quickly. Accepting credit cards also expedited my order processing and shipping. Orders for my credit card customers typically ship within 24 hours of placement. Beat that, Egghead! All it took to reap this bonanza was the placement of the billboard shown in Figure 19.1 at the top of my auction ads.

To defray the merchant account's 2.3 percent plus 30-cent transaction fee, I increased the price of each product by one dollar across the line, credit card payment or not.

Figure 19.1 *Cyber-sales with the click of the mouse*

You may be asking how I can lambaste BillPoint in the same breath that I recommend a merchant account. The difference between BillPoint—or PayPal for that matter—and a merchant account is like the difference between real money and Bingo money: you can only spend Bingo money in the Bingo parlor! To use BillPoint or PayPal you must first register. The vast majority of Web surfers have never heard of BillPoint or PayPal, and the majority of those who have aren't registered. I'm not putting e-pay down. I'm suggesting that its scope may be much narrower than its proponents would like to believe.

Plastic Cards and Shopping Carts

Accepting plastic not only increased my auction sales, it made my Web site practical. BC—*before cards*—it was only a pilot light, a glimmering of possibilities. With the addition of the real-time "shopping cart" that came with my merchant account my Web site became interactive (see Figure 19.2). If the fancy now strikes somebody to lay down plastic on of my products they click, my shopping cart tallies their purchase, and they're whisked to a secure payment gateway where their credit card and shipping info are recorded. The proceeds are wired into my bank account 48 hours later. The advantage of accepting credit cards is that my Web site is now open for business 24/7 in all time zones.

The Merchant Account Pyramid

Finding an Internet merchant account is easy. Simply enter the keywords *merchant account* in any major search engine and you'll get dozens of hits. Finding a competent merchant bank with low transaction fees packaged with a well-priced real-time payment gateway is considerably harder.

Unfortunately, merchant accounts are one of the biggest Ponzi schemes—a.k.a. multi-level-marketing plans, a.k.a. affiliate networks—on the Internet. If you were to apply for a merchant account through Quick Commerce Solutions by logging onto http://www.qcaffiliate.com/qc/zenweb /index.html, for example, I'd pocket a $75 commission (see Figure 19.3).

Here's how the merchant account pyramid breaks down from top to bottom.

1. **The merchant bank**. At the top of the pyramid is a bank that underwrites your creditworthiness as a business. This bank is the conduit for all of your credit card transactions. It receives money from your payment gateway and deposits the funds electronically in your personal bank account.

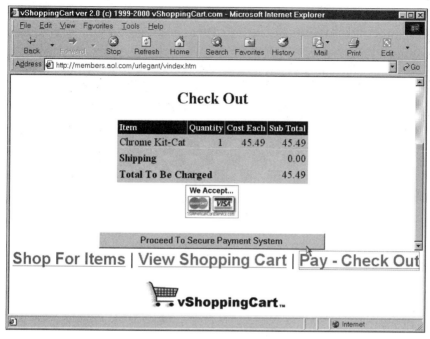

Figure 19.2 *My shopping cart*

Figure 19.3 *Won't you step into my parlor?*

2. **The secure payment gateway.** The payment gateway is a secure Web site where transactions are recorded in real time and submitted to the credit card company for approval.

3. **The merchant account broker.** The account broker or reseller is a middleman between you (as the applicant) and the merchant bank. The account broker packages the deal. They sell you on the merchant account while selling the merchant bank on you. They also set the price!

4. **The merchant account affiliate**. An agent for the account broker, the affiliate drives merchant account prospects to the broker for a commission.

What to Look for in a Merchant Bank

Most commercial banks can't compete with a merchant bank that specializes in Internet commerce. I paid a one-time fee of $465 to First American Credit Card Services, a broker for Authorize.net, my payment gateway, and the National Bank of the Redwoods, my merchant bank. Compare that with Bank of America, which charges a one-time setup fee of $250 plus an ongoing monthly fee of $100 for a comparable real-time shopping cart system. I rest my case. Here are the salient points to negotiate.

➤ **Gateway license**. I paid a one-time all-inclusive licensing fee of $465 for my Authorize.net account. This fee also covered the broker's commission.

➤ **Real-time shopping cart.** Avoid stripped-down merchant accounts that don't process credit card transactions in real time. A merchant account without a shopping cart is like a car without wheels. I paid $50 for an option called Weblink, which links my customers directly to a secure Authorize.net payment gateway. Weblink works with V-ShoppingCart, a reliable, easy-to-program shopping cart that tallies my customers' orders and processes their transactions in real time. Weblink and V-Shopping-Cart were both included in my $465 payment.

➤ **Monthly fees**. I pay $9 for each monthly statement; you shouldn't pay more than that.

➤ **Transaction fees**. I pay 30 cents per transaction plus a bank discount rate of 2.3 percent per transaction.

➤ **Hidden costs**. You should never have to pay a setup or application fee.

➤ **Lease**. You can pay off a merchant account over time but it will cost you. A recurring $25 a month over 48 months will cost you $1200 for the same package for which I paid $465. Buy a merchant account in one lump sum for the lowest price you can find. And remember—it's a tax write-off!

Fly-by-Nighters

Offering Internet merchant accounts is a dog-eat-dog business and there are many shoddy operations trying to take advantage of it. Stay near the top of the pyramid! Deal only with authorized merchant account brokers and resellers. Avoid bottom-feeders like affiliates and sub-agents. You may be able to negotiate a better deal than mine, but you shouldn't pay a penny more.

I've had mostly positive experiences with Authorize.net. Log on to http://www.authorizenet.com for a list of authorized resellers. Another good site to shop for merchant accounts is http://www.onlineorders.net. It's devoted to evaluating merchant accounts and shopping cart software and contains useful links and information. Be advised that this site is advertising-supported and many of their reviews are of advertisers. You'll find these URLs and more on the *Confessions* CD-ROM under Marketing Tools/Merchant Services.

Slicing up the Budget Pie

The time has come to rethink the economics of your enterprise. With Internet auctions and a Web site to promote, you must determine how to manage your budget to attract maximum sales at minimum price. Featured auctions, search engine submission, banner advertising, a merchant account—it takes money to make money. How much are you willing to invest in yourself? That's the bottom line.

To put my own spin on McLuhan's metaphor, credit cards are like a nondenominational faith. If you have one, you belong. If you accept them, you're the Church!

CHAPTER 20

The Eighth Continent: The State Of Cyberspace

"Today, after more than a century of electric technology, we have extended our central nervous system itself in a global embrace, abolishing both space and time as far as our planet is concerned."
—Marshall McLuhan, *Understanding Media: The Extensions of Man* (1964)

Europe, Asia, Africa, North America, South America, Antarctica, Australia, the Internet? The advent of the Internet is no less profound than the discovery a new continent. For all intents and purposes the Internet is the Earth's eighth continent!

Conventional wisdom cites the invention of the printing press by Johann Gutenberg, around 1450, as the breakthrough that sparked mass communication. On March 10, 1876, as Alexander Graham Bell and his assistant, Thomas A. Watson, were preparing to test Bell's newly patented "voice transmitter-receiver," Bell spilled some acid on himself. In another room Watson, who was sitting next to the receiver, clearly heard the world's first telephone message: "Mr. Watson, come here; I want you." No breakthrough since the invention of the printing press over 400 years earlier would facilitate mankind's ability to communicate more profoundly than the telephone. Until the Internet.

The Third Wave

The Internet is the third wave of the Communications Revolution. This doesn't negate the importance of radio, television, satellites, or the personal computer. In the future they will all be vital components of the Internet.

The Internet began as a Cold War technology, a way for military computers to communicate over long distances. In the 1970s and 1980s other institutions, universities and hospitals, began linking their computers together through the Internet, too. Consumers and commercial enterprises got in on the act with the development of the World Wide Web in 1989.

According to Microsoft Encarta, "The Internet promises to be the nervous system of the global village, a crucial pathway in the exchange of information. Already, in its early stages, the Internet is transmitting information nearly instantaneously from one point on the globe to the other, leaping across oceans, racing over borders, and crossing cultural and social boundaries. Its effects are impossible to predict, but if history is any guide, it promises to transform the world—for better or worse—as profoundly as the printing press did more than 500 years ago." Who should know better than Microsoft?

Revisionist History

I think the pundits and historians have gotten it wrong. I believe Bill Gates was far more responsible for the booming economy of the 1990s than Bill Clinton was. I'm not discounting the given genius of Alan Greenspan or Robert Rubin. My hypothesis is simply that without Microsoft there would have been no technology boom. Without a technology boom there would have been no NASDAQ boom. Without a NASDAQ boom there would have been no stock market boom. And without a stock market boom there would have been no economic boom. In my perspective you can trace the current state of America's booming economy directly back to the release of Microsoft Windows 3.1, in 1991!

I'm writing this book using Corel WordPerfect even though I have Microsoft Word. My database and PIM is Commence even though I have Microsoft Outlook and Access. I use Corel Photo-Paint even though I have Adobe Photo Deluxe and Microsoft Photo Editor. Would you say these products are better or worse due to competition from Microsoft? I can definitively declare they're better! Would you say they're more or less expensive? They're definitely less expensive. So how have I, the consumer, been hurt by Microsoft? I haven't. I've benefited by being able to exercise choice. Microsoft didn't quell competition in the software industry. On the contrary, it stimulated it!

The NASDAQ meltdown of spring 2000 had far less to do with Alan Greenspan's tightening the screws on inflation than the Justice Department's unjust triumph over Microsoft in the courts. History may prove me wrong, but I'm going to go out on a limb. Maybe this is wishful thinking—but I don't think Microsoft will be broken up. Ultimately, I think Bill Gates will prevail by winning a reversal on appeal. Microsoft's alleged predatory practices were in fact no less predatory than the hardball played by the competition. At most they merit a slap on the wrist. To quote Dennis Miller, "That's only my opinion and I might be wrong!"

Merger Mania

During one frantic week of wheeling and dealing in mid-December 1999, America Online entered into two multimillion dollar pacts—with Circuit City and Wal-Mart—one day after Yahoo! entered into a similar pact with Kmart and Microsoft invested $200 million in Best Buy. The pundits christened it "Click-and-Brick." A month later "Click-and-Brick" was dead and B2B (business to business) was in. A few months after that, AOL announced it was acquiring Time-Warner and merger mania was back on Wall Street. CNBC was stuttering.

During the previous year, NBC joined forces with Microsoft, Ted Turner rolled CNN into Time-Warner, Michael Eisner bought ABC for Mickey Mouse, and Mel Karmazin sold CBS to Sumner Redstone's Viacom. The only remaining question is who will merge with Barry Diller?

These media, Internet, and retail titans all formed alliances for a single reason: fear! The Internet is too vast for anyone alone to conquer. And nobody knows how it's going to shake out.

The Internet World Trade Show

A seemingly eternal multitude of registrants queued up like lambs going to slaughter. I was attending Internet World, the industry's hottest trade show; it was like being transported to another planet. Tens of thousands of people slowly zigzagged their way to hundreds of computer terminals in never-ending banks. From beginning to end it took less than half an hour to get there, a miracle considering over a hundred thousand people were in attendance. The line and registration process itself was self-perpetuating and entirely self-participatory. When I arrived at the computer terminal I registered myself in a matter of seconds and was directed to a printing kiosk. From there, an HP LaserJet 5000 spit out my badge and I hit the floor running.

What Planet Is This?

What planet is this? I thought to myself, as I wandered down an aisle in the first of several exhibit halls. This was the biggest, splashiest, richest computer show this side of COMDEX and I couldn't figure out what half of these companies were selling. I was somewhat relieved to discover many of the exhibitors themselves couldn't explain what they were selling!

Several technologies hadn't even been released yet; the industry term for this is *vaporware*. Computer technology changes so rapidly that it's anybody's guess what the future will bring. Half of these upstarts with no products to sell are already owned by major conglomerates, underscoring the merger mania previously discussed. Giant corporations are placing their bets on the future of the Internet as if it were a giant roulette wheel. Meanwhile, I have a hard time explaining to my mother how I earn more money selling Kit-Cat clocks than Amazon does selling books.

The Death of Moore's Law

It seems like it was only yesterday that I scoffed at Larry Ellison and Scott McNealy of Oracle and Sun for proclaiming the demise of the PC to Charlie Rose. Now I'm convinced even our toilet seats will be connected to the Internet in the future.

The name *Intel* was derived by combining the words *int*egrated and *el*ectronics. Intel was founded in 1968 by engineers Gordon Moore and Bob Noyce, who left Fairchild Semiconductor to form their own company. They were soon joined by Andy Grove, who became Intel's president. Gordon Moore once predicted that the number of transistors contained on a computer chip, and hence its speed, would double every 18 months. This became known as Moore's Law and it was accurate until a few years ago.

I currently have all the speed I need. My three-year-old 300MHz Pentium 2 with its high-resolution 19-inch monitor and Digital Dolby Surround Sound speakers rivals the fastest Athalons and Pentium 3s of today. How fast can you blink? That's the difference in speed between old and new. The unwritten part of Moore's Law was that you had to upgrade your computer every 18 months, too, because PCs were so slow. Not anymore! I do dream of someday upgrading to Intel's new 64-bit Itanium processor with a 21-inch flat panel LCD display—maybe when the 2GHz models dip below $2,002. That'll probably be in 2002. For now I have all the speed I need and Moore's Law is out the window. The PC isn't dead. It's transforming itself into a door knob.

Fools Rush in

The most heavily trafficked commerce site on the Internet last Christmas was eBay. It cost a mere 25 cents to join the party. I must have sold close to a hundred Kit-Cat clocks last Christmas on eBay alone. That's raw empowerment! Will eBay remain the 800-pound gorilla of Internet auction business? No legitimate challenger has appeared on the horizon during the course of writing this book. All I can state with relative certainty is that Internet auctions are here to stay and I've been fortunate to derive a lucrative income from them.

My Kit-Cat clock sales generate four or five hours a week in labor, and I earn $75 to $150 for each of those hours. I've auctioned other product lines that have sold equally well. Internet auctions can produce a nice cash flow, but they'll never make you rich. I realized a long time ago that I'm not in Internet auctions for the money. I dig them for the experience. I'm a recovering Internet auction junkie—that's why I wrote this book.

A Minute Past Midnight

It's a minute past midnight. The Internet revolution has barely begun. The train hasn't even left the station yet. It's not too late to climb aboard. Internet auctions are the caboose. You may stay there if you like, or work your way forward to the club car where you can become the next garage millionaire. Whatever you decide, thanks for coming along on the ride. God bless you and good luck!

Index

G

general categories, 61–62
GIF file format, 88
greenbacks, 122
Greenspan, Alan, 241
grids, creating (in ads), 84
group purchase auctions, 210
guides, selling, 177–179

H

headlines
    character limits, 29–30
    conciseness, 29–30
    counting characters, 111–112
    persuasiveness, 33–34
    prohibited words, 72–73
    searchability, 30, 32–33
    size, 97
    successful, characteristics of,
        29
Hirsch, Arthur, 184, 186,
    189–190
Hirsch, Eileen, 184, 186,
    189–190
home page, setting auction page
    as, 133–134
HTM file format, 88
HTML (HyperText Markup
    Language), 78
    editors, 78–79
        Alignment icons, 83
        Edit icons, 80
        File icons, 80
        formatting text, 80–81
        Image icons, 80
        List icons, 86–88
        Page Attributes icons, 83

Table icons, 84–86
file formats, 88
META tags, 228
source code, viewing, 91–92
TITLE tags, 227–228
tutorials, 106

I

iCAT Mall, 160–161
images (in ads)
    adding, 80
    aligning, 83
    Amazon and Yahoo! ads,
        115–116
    borders, 84
    compressing, 106
    copying from other pages,
        93–94
    FTP space, 88–89, 114–115
    obtaining, 104
    resizing, 105–106
    uploading, 89–91, 112–113
impression fees (banner ads), 229
information, selling, 177–179
Ingram Micro (wholesaler),
    199–202
inherent value, finding, 76
insurance, 50
Intel, 243
Internet
    as communications revolution,
        240–241
    compared to printing press,
        241
    as economic stimulator, 241
    history of, 240
    new technologies, 242–243

The Ultimate
Online Auction Experience... X 4!

Starting Your Online Auction Business
0-7615-2921-7 ▪ U.S. $24.99
Can.$37.95 ▪ U.K. £18.99
Available:
December 2000

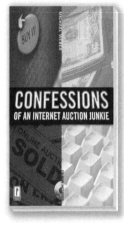

Confessions of an Internet Auction Junkie
0-7615-3085-1 ▪ U.S. $29.99
Can. $44.95 ▪ U.K. £21.99
Available:
October 2000

Online Auctions at eBay, 2nd Edition
0-7615-2414-2 ▪ U.S. $19.99
Can. $29.95 ▪ U.K. £14.99
Now Available!

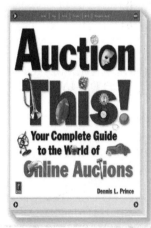

Auction This! Your Complete Guide to the World of Online Auctions
0-7615-2316-2 ▪ U.S. $19.99
Can. $29.95 ▪ U.K. £14.99
Now Available!

License Agreement/Notice of Limited Warranty

By opening the sealed disk container in this book, you agree to the following terms and conditions. If, upon reading the following license agreement and notice of limited warranty, you cannot agree to the terms and conditions set forth, return the unused book with unopened disk to the place where you purchased it for a refund.

License:

The enclosed software is copyrighted by the copyright holder(s) indicated on the software disk. You are licensed to copy the software onto a single computer for use by a single concurrent user and to a backup disk. You may not reproduce, make copies, or distribute copies or rent or lease the software in whole or in part, except with written permission of the copyright holder(s). You may transfer the enclosed disk only together with this license, and only if you destroy all other copies of the software and the transferee agrees to the terms of the license. You may not decompile, reverse assemble, or reverse engineer the software.

Notice of Limited Warranty:

The enclosed disk is warranted by Prima Publishing to be free of physical defects in materials and workmanship for a period of sixty (60) days from end user's purchase of the book/disk combination. During the sixty-day term of the limited warranty, Prima will provide a replacement disk upon the return of a defective disk.

Limited Liability:

THE SOLE REMEDY FOR BREACH OF THIS LIMITED WARRANTY SHALL CONSIST ENTIRELY OF REPLACEMENT OF THE DEFECTIVE DISK. IN NO EVENT SHALL PRIMA OR THE AUTHORS BE LIABLE FOR ANY OTHER DAMAGES, INCLUDING LOSS OR CORRUPTION OF DATA, CHANGES IN THE FUNCTIONAL CHARACTERISTICS OF THE HARDWARE OR OPERATING SYSTEM, DELETERIOUS INTERACTION WITH OTHER SOFTWARE, OR ANY OTHER SPECIAL, INCIDENTAL, OR CONSEQUENTIAL DAMAGES THAT MAY ARISE, EVEN IF PRIMA AND/OR THE AUTHOR HAVE PREVIOUSLY BEEN NOTIFIED THAT THE POSSIBILITY OF SUCH DAMAGES EXISTS.

Disclaimer of Warranties:

PRIMA AND THE AUTHORS SPECIFICALLY DISCLAIM ANY AND ALL OTHER WARRANTIES, EITHER EXPRESS OR IMPLIED, INCLUDING WARRANTIES OF MERCHANTABILITY, SUITABILITY TO A PARTICULAR TASK OR PURPOSE, OR FREEDOM FROM ERRORS. SOME STATES DO NOT ALLOW FOR EXCLUSION OF IMPLIED WARRANTIES OR LIMITATION OF INCIDENTAL OR CONSEQUENTIAL DAMAGES, SO THESE LIMITATIONS MAY NOT APPLY TO YOU.

Other:

This Agreement is governed by the laws of the State of California without regard to choice of law principles. The United Convention of Contracts for the International Sale of Goods is specifically disclaimed. This Agreement constitutes the entire agreement between you and Prima Publishing regarding use of the software.